PSI NATIONAL REAL ESTATE LICENSE EXAM PREP

The Most Complete Study Guide to Pass the Exam With Ease | Includes Real Estate Core Concepts, Math Calculations, 250 Up-To-Date Questions and Strategies

Ashton Kingsley

Disclaimer

This publication is designed to provide accurate and authoritative information in regard to the subject matter covered. It is sold with the understanding that neither the author nor the publisher is engaged in rendering legal, investment, accounting or other professional services.

While the publisher and author have used their best efforts in preparing this book, they make no representations or warranties with respect to the accuracy or completeness of the contents of this book and specifically disclaim any implied warranties of merchantability or fitness for a particular purpose. No warranty may be created or extended by sales representatives or written sales materials. The advice and strategies contained herein may not be suitable for your situation. You should consult with a professional when appropriate. Neither the publisher nor the author shall be liable for any loss of profit or any other commercial damages, including but not limited to special, incidental, consequential, personal, or other damages.

CONTENTS

1. Overview of the PSI Real Estate National License Exam

Knowing about something is important. Being certified about something is rare!

Welcome on your journey of becoming a certified agent and start your career as a successful Salesperson.

The PSI Real Estate certification is valid across most of the states and once you have obtained the license you can start practicing professionally. It's an exam where a detailed assessment of a candidate's knowledge in various fields and aspects of real estate is tested. Before taking the exam you have to make sure that you have completed the 60 hours salesperson pre-education. You shall arrive minimum 30 minutes earlier to your appointment time on your examination day in order to make the sign-in, identification process and familiarize yourself with the examination process. Don't forget to bring with you the 2 requested forms of identification: as primary identification you can bring: State issued driver's license, Identification Card, US Issued Passport or Military Identification Card, as well as an US Government Issued Alien Registration card. As secondary identification document you can use any signed Debit or Credit Card as well as a wholesale store card. The exam will have a positive outcome if you reach a minimum of 75% correct answers.

Just to share with you, the gateway of opportunities for a certified salesperson is open for all. In today's digital world, there are more than one way of finding clients, especially through social media.

While that is the latter part, our goal with this book is to prepare you not alone for the exam, but for whatever is coming ahead after that when you have passed it and you now deal with a multitude of clients. You are now setting free from the financial barriers.

Before we move ahead, let's prepare you with tips for the ideal mindset that will help you immensely.

2. Study Tips & Strategies for Positive Results

Success in the PSI Real Estate exam doesn't happen by chance; it requires a well-thought-out study schedule that maximizes your preparation time. Creating a personalized study plan ensures that you reach your destination of PSI Real Estate certification with confidence.

Take a moment to review your learning style and life circumstances. Are you most concentrated studying during the morning hours, or do you find yourself more focused during evening studies? Do you work, have family, or other responsibilities that will influence the time you can dedicate to studying? These factors are essential in creating a realistic and effective study plan.

Once you have a clear understanding of your availability and personal learning preferences, it's time to break down the PSI Real Estate exam content areas. The exam covers several domains: Property ownership, Land use control and regulations, Valuation and market analysis, Financing, General principles of agency, Property disclosure, contracts, Leasing and Property Management, Transfer of Title, Practice of real estate and Real Estate calculations. Each subject needs careful consideration and should be allocated time in your study schedule based on your level of familiarity with the material.

You should try to familiarize yourself with the exam format and structure by taking practice tests under timed conditions to be prepared for the real exam. It could help to develop your own way of tackling multiple-choice questions, such as making sure that your incorrect answers are getting lower per every mock test or sample exam you give.

As an example of diligent planning, let's create a hypothetical four-week schedule leading up to the exam:

Weeks 1-2: Focus on the most challenging content areas for you. If Real Estate calculations are difficult for you, allocate larger blocks of time towards it. Use these first weeks to build a strong foundation in the areas that require more effort.

Week 3: Start integrating practice questions related to the content you have covered in Weeks 1-2. This will help solidify your knowledge and identify any gaps. Simultaneously begin reviewing all the other topics.

Week 4: Dedicate this week to review all the content areas while continuing to answer practice questions. End the week with full-length practice exams to simulate test conditions.

Here are additional tips as you structure your daily study sessions:

1. **Be specific with your goals for each session:** instead of planning to "study Real Estate Math", set an objective like "understand the differences between the various types of loans."

2. **Incorporate different learning methods:** read textbooks, watch informational videos, create flashcards for memorization, or engage in discussion groups.

3. **Build in short breaks:** studying for an hour followed by a 10-minute break can help maintain focus and improve retention.

4. **Be consistent with study times:** studying at regular intervals helps establish a routine conducive to effective learning.

5. **Keep track of progress:** at the end of each day or week, evaluate what was accomplished and adjust as necessary.

6. **Make room for buffer time:** unforeseen events can happen; having spare time in your schedule allows adjustments without stress.

Always remember that quality is better than quantity—spending hours passively reading may not be as productive as an intense focused session using active recall methods like teaching back or self-quizzing.

Lastly, practice self-care throughout your preparation time. Sleep, nutrition, exercise, and relaxation are not only crucial for maintaining health but also directly impact cognitive function essential for successful exam performance.

Creating your optimal study schedule for PSI Real Estate exam prep isn't just about allocating time; it's about strategy and knowing yourself as a learner. Stick with it consistently yet flexibly, making necessary changes along the way due to performance data or life's demands, and march confidently towards achieving certification.

You need to review at regular intervals, so that you know where you are heading, and which sections or chapters need the most attention. In the end, you should prioritize understanding the concepts instead of memorizing the content. As you will see in the upcoming chapters, we have tried our best to focus on critical thinking and application of knowledge rather than simple recalling, as that will get you nowhere.

In the end, throughout the contents of this book, you will find a discussion on all the key components that are included in the syllabus of this exam. Also, this refers to all the faces of the world that is coming ahead, of real estate. From a mere definition of real properties to detailed laws about discrimination, this book will take you on an enticing journey.

We have tried our best not to make this boring or old-school academic book. All of the concepts have been illustrated by the usage of a communicative team as if we were talking to you.

We hope that you enjoy the contents of this meticulously designed guide. Rest assured, let's jump straight into exploring different factors and topics that you need to know to become a successful real estate agent.

A quick reminder: Throughout this book, we will focus on grasping the concepts instead of the imagination of being rich all the time, and making big money. There is no time for that. Our goal as a real estate agent should not be to earn cash for ourselves but to generate and add value to the whole market.

Let's begin!

Chapter 1

PROPERTY OWNERSHIP

The foremost thing that one needs to understand in the world of estates and properties is the underlying legal definitions which will empower you to hold a firm grip over the core concepts, further uplifting your ability to clarify your case and offer when you start your career as a professional real estate agent.

It is important to note here that in day-to-day language, we might be referring to properties using words that are common in nature. For example, one might refer to a piece of land somewhere or a building as real estate in general. A person who deals in this kind of business might be referred to as a real estate agent.

However, the differences start to appear when we explore the same question/referrals through another set of languages: legal language.

In the professional side of any industry, whether it's estate or big tech, even the slightest misunderstanding can result in a larger conflict which can threaten the future, making the legitimacy of your contract vulnerable. When we talk to someone, it is easier for us to illustrate or convey our meaning, let's call that conversation for now. You are free to choose any set of words or sentences to make your deal or communicate information.

But when it comes to paperwork and the legal side of the business, it is very important to focus on mentioning the right set of words because even the slightest change (as you will see in the next section) can pose greater barriers for both you and your possible clients.

Without further ado, let's jump straight into defining the power of words in this world of estate and properties.

A. Personal vs Real Properties

We live in a world full of taxation and legal evaluations. Therefore, as a real estate agent, your first goal should be to become one who is trustworthy, has a good reputation, and works to assist his/her clients. You can call it a matter of goodwill or creating value for your clients, whether they are willing to buy or sell off their properties, both of which will determine the scope of your success.

But goodwill alone isn't enough. You need to understand the underlying complexities to gain command over yourself or your knowledge of properties.

Now, there are two kinds of properties.

One is personal. And the other one is real.

Starting from personal property, anything that is movable (except land) can be regarded as personal property. Another way to express this would be "Anything that is not attached to the property and can be moved easily is personal."

For example, you get a buyer who is looking to buy a nice house for a family of three. You make your search and find a seller whose agent takes you all on a tour of a house. It's a well-decorated house, fully furnished, with some nice sofas and a TV. Your client likes the house and is excited that he won't have to worry much about the future, so he is ready to buy.

The deal is closed but when he moves in, he finds out that there is no furniture within. Now, that's a problem because the buyer might have agreed to a price that the seller wanted just because he thought that it would be easier for him to set up his house, and start a joyous family.

Speaking of that, does there exist any legal action that he can take against the seller? The answer is no!

Any property that is not attached to the house is personal. Even the wood and material used for construction or anything else is personal until it has been laid down in the ground to construct.

But a chandelier or blindfolds that are attached to the house are not personal.

Now that you know what a personal property is. It is very effortless for you to understand what real property is. Let's define it quickly:

"Land, plus anything that is immovable and is attached to the property is real. The same planks that were personal, when they were laid down to the foundation (attached), are now called real property."

For example, the same chandelier, or a tree, or maybe a dog house. But if the house that your client was willing to buy comes with some nice decorated flower pots, then that's personal property and unless both buyers and sellers have agreed to what they will be able to keep, there is no set of legal action that can be taken against them in case the seller decides to take their personal property with them.

Now that you know the underlying differences between personal and real properties, let's define the key takeaways from here:

- It is important to understand the vitality of how a slight misuse of a word can pose sufficient problems for you.

- Communicative language is different from legal language.

- The taxations work differently for personal and real properties so one must seek a financial advisor (we will cover more of it in the coming chapters) so that your credibility as an agent who makes legit deals is maintained.

A Quick Question – What is a conveyance in real estate?

Well, the same deal or transfer of ownership rights of real property from a buyer to a seller. It can be a home, or just land, or a whole building. You can call this an agreement between those two parties (buyer and seller) which defines the mutual agreement between them.

It is important that before any conveyance is made, you must ask your party (whether buyer or seller) questions related to how the personal property will be settled. One important tip here is to educate your clients on the implications (as we had seen in a previous misunderstanding where the seller took all of their personal property) of a slight difference in legal language.

Also, bring them onto a mutual agreement as to how and who will take the personal properties so you don't have to worry about disputes arising later.

With that being said, let's delve deeper into this world of legal descriptions. You should be assured that you are going to find a nice and detailed discussion plus notes in whatever is coming up next. It has been made sure that you get an inclusive and insightful overview of everything, all of the topics, that you will need to pass your PSI Real Estate Exam Test.

As we have successfully repeated the word "real" once again, we shall remind you of one basic yet very important lesson that we have learned up till now. It entails a basic yet important lesson that you might someday be proud of or you might be uttering it in front of your grandchildren, telling them stories of where you started from and all that you have experienced in your journey!

We will try our best to keep it as communicative as we can because it's human nature and wisdom that information is both accepted and conveyed in its best form when it's easier to. Our minds are such powerful, the way they can work, and produce, it's beyond explanation.

Now, that's too much of stories and some ideas that are more related to the subconscious mind. And they are necessary to know to gain the maximum output from this book.

Let's now quickly cover a few important topics that are related to property ownership.

B. Land Characteristics and Legal Descriptions

As it sounds, Land Characteristics refer to several features of the land, that help you determine the exact value of it. These features can be multiple, depending on the scale of how much you are willing to define the attributes of the land. A wise approach here is that the deeper we dig in, the better gems we find.

These are the things that land characteristics can have. But you can use your imagination to think of as many as you can and note them down somewhere. There are always endless possibilities:

- **Location –** *You will already know that it is a very crucial factor. The location is important because your clients can have different preferences, everyone lives a different life. There are a few things that all of them want in common. We can call them needs. To describe a location, you could analyze if it is close to a station, or a school, or if it is a nice apartment that can fit a model or a celebrity. All These are directly related to the value of land or real property.*

- **Topography –** *The natural features of the property of land. If it's land, is it on a slope, what's the elevation of a property, or is the house built on a strong foundation that can withstand extreme conditions? Also, it is unrelated to the natural features, but*

- **Soil Quality –** *the quality of the soil determines the purpose that land can be used for such as its suitability for agriculture. Or construction?*

- **Features and Infrastructures –** *How's the access to the land? Is it easier to reach? Also, these questions can help you show your clients what is the most ideal thing that they can do at their land. If it's around a space where you think development can occur in the coming years, then how about reserving it for some nice commercial activity while for now, you can cultivate something? The population has to grow and everyone needs land. It is simple. It also includes things like environmental factors or some land regulations.*

- **Size and Shape – (more about this in legal descriptions)**

It is always important to know as many features, attributes, and things that define you, and when you mention all of these in front of your future clients, would they be able to imagine it?

So, we have a question here that you can answer for yourself:

"Do you agree that one can increase the chances of closing their client and express desirability, plus as a value addition, that same person can show their clients a future perspective that is backed by sufficient research, and that makes them profitable? Is it possible?"

Now, if your answer was "yes", you might want to hear our explanation.

We think the same. One can close more clients by adopting these factors whilst engaging with them:

1. If an agent presents a property in a desirable manner, highlighting its main features and characteristics, potential, amenities, and other benefits through the use of desirable language, then they can close most of their clients.

2. If an agent details the client about the future prospects of a society and explains all the benefits to them can facilitate their decision-making, their chances of closing them are definitely more than if the agent was not to do that. This can include market analysis, trend forecasts, opportunities, and potential risks.

3. In the end, if an agent focuses on good research where all the essential factors and aspects of the property or client requirements are examined and results are drawn and communicated to the client, then it is very likely that they would like to close the deal. Because they would be able to see your dedication and good analytical skills, which can be a great value addition for the agent and client.

A Quick Activity!

Take out a sheet of paper from your notebook and write here in 3 sentences that you think you will use as a real estate agent if you were selling your property.

----

1 – Types of Legal Descriptions

Legal descriptions relate to the exact measurements and location. Note that, you are not to confuse address with location because addresses are common in nature. And because it's a legal description, so this precise location is what will be mentioned when the property is being transferred.

Also, some vacant lots often come with no addresses. That's why location solves all of the disputes that can arise when rights are being transferred from a buyer to a seller.

Legal descriptions have several types such as:

Metes and Bounds

Metes refers to distance and direction while Bounds (as it sounds) refer to the boundary of a real property or land. It is one of the oldest methods that were used by the English, but it is still practical as of today.

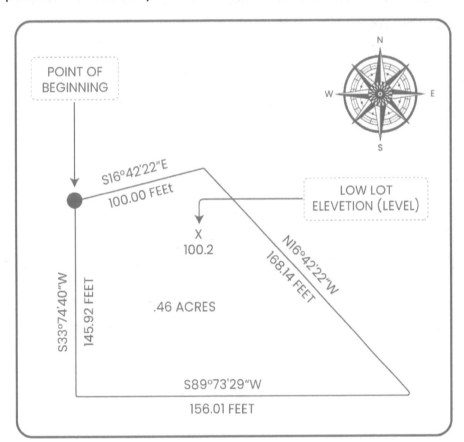

It can include:

- Specifying boundary lines and angles of a property.

- References to natural objects like rocks, trees, water (river or stream)

- References to artificial objects such as bridges.

Plat/Lot & Block

This is a method that is mostly used today. It is currently serving different modern communities across the world, also commercial setups, and industrial areas.

Let us try to illustrate this merely.

A plat is a record. That will be stored as legal and will help determine the precise location, one which is mentioned when rights are transferred.

Now to plan better, our civilizations now follow this method where we divide a piece of land into lots and blocks.

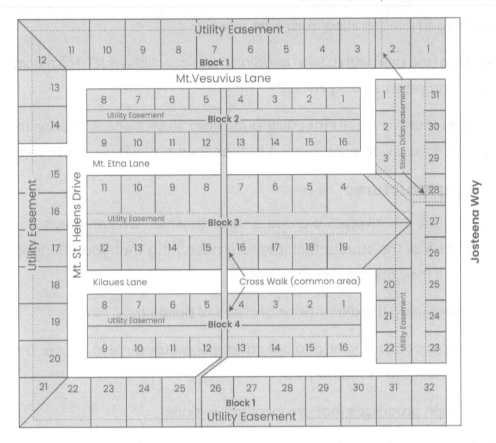

You can see above an illustration of blocks 1 to 4 with several lots.

In every plat, there is a central point that we use as a reference. It can be anything from a monument to anything that helps the surveyor (one who maintains the record in the property's jurisdiction) determine the precise location and add it to the record book of the respective property's record or map.

Now, you know how modern cities are planned. A multitude of plats.

Government Surveys

This is used by governments (state and federal) to divide the land into townships and ranges. Now these are plotted on a grid and contain:

- **Meridian** (the grid line running from north to south)

- **Principal Meridian** (The midpoint in the grid line that divides the east from the west)

- **Parallel** (grid lines running from east to west)

- **Township** (the area within two meridians and parallels which form a square, each of which represents 36 sq. miles)

- **Sections** (A township is further distributed into 36 sections, with each representing 1 sq. mile. If we divide each section further, then that will be a sub-section.)

2 - Measuring Structures

As the term implies, this involves a process through which we can measure all kinds of real property. It's just the square feet, the foremost thing that you will need to inquire from your client if they are a buyer or a seller.

It's the art of measuring the dimensions and size of buildings.

Keep in mind that not all kinds of land are square or rectangular in shape. Therefore, not all structures are square or rectangular.

The most common processes that are involved in it are:

- **Exterior and Interior Measurements:** *The exterior measurements involve measuring the height, length, and width of the exterior perimeter of a building. If it's a house, then you can start from where the walls are!*

- *Similarly, interior measurements include measuring the building from the inside. For example, you can measure the size of rooms and their dimensions to understand how much space exists inside of the property. The better your assessment is, the better will be your pitch.*

- **Measuring in the most common format:** *The square footage. You can measure this simply by multiplying the length of a room with its width. Now, if there are 4 rooms, then you can add the sum of these 4 to get the total area that it covers.*

- **Blueprints and 3D modeling:** *Blueprints can help you immensely, providing you with details about the layout of walls, how the structure looks, and the overall size* and dimensions. You can take this to an advanced level by using 3D modeling software to get more insights about the property.

- **Ask a Professional:** *In case you want a professional output or assessment, you can just hire one or offer a partnership to them. You will need it the most when you are looking to evaluate the design of the structure and space within. The better your assessment is, the more money you will be able to save. And that means more profits.*

3 - Livable, Usable, and Rentable Area

Since we were already talking about space and evaluating it in case our client wants to modify it as per their needs, let's briefly see how we can distinguish space so that we have more insights.

- **Livable Area:** *This includes places suitable for living such as living rooms, bedrooms, dining rooms, kitchens, and furnished basements. Any space where we can live.*

  We can't live on stairs so we might exclude it from our calculation of livable area. The same goes for hallways or car porches.

- **Usable Area:** *As the name implies, usable area relates to any area that can be utilized for some purpose. It can be a garden or a garage.*

  Also, it can be a storage room, balconies, patio, or just anything that can be utilized for some purpose.

- **Rentable Area:** *Any area that can be rented. It can include a livable area, a usable area, or both. Just anything that can be rented to tenants.*

Now that we know how to measure structures, or the factors that we can keep in mind when measuring a building, we also need to explore a little about how land is measured.

4 - Land Measurements

The land is measured in several formats, that change slightly depending on the geographic region of the world. These are some of the units and measurement insights that you will need to know before getting a land measured.

- **Square Footage (sq ft):** *As previously discussed, this is a common unit for measuring land.*

- **Square Meters (sq m):** *It is also used widely throughout the world. As the word implies, one square meter is equal to a square that is one meter long on all of its sides.*

- **Acre:** *We hear a lot about acre mentioned here and there especially when it's a good agricultural land that is up for selling because the seller needs instant liquidity. 1 acre (in the US) is equivalent to 43,560 sq ft or roughly 4,047 sq meters.*

- **Hectare:** *It is often used in properties that are agricultural or lie on the rural side. 1 hectare is equivalent to 2.47 acres or 10,000 sq meters.*

- **Square Yards:** *A few properties are also measured in square yards, especially in regions like the United Kingdom, India, and Pakistan. It is mainly used for residential plots as well as for commercial properties.*

Now, there is another system used by the government to administer land measurements and control. It is known as the **Rectangular Government Survey System (RGSS)** or **Public Land Survey System (PLSS)**.

It works by dividing a land into small square patches so that it is easier to identify each one. Its layout and division of sections work in this way:

a. **Layout:** *Its map layout as many other methods exist of a grid system which is formed by drawing intersecting lines (principal meridians & baselines). The principal meridian lines are north-south lines while baselines are east-west lines. The point where these two lines intersect is called the initial point from which the* grid extends in both directions with squares and rectangular patches forming in perfect symmetry (north-south to east-west).

b. **Division of Sections:** *RGSS's primary unit for land measurement is a section. Each section represents one square mile of land or around 640 acres which is divided into standard sections numbered from 1 to 36. In the end, if a quarter-section term is being used somewhere, then it represents some 160 acres.*

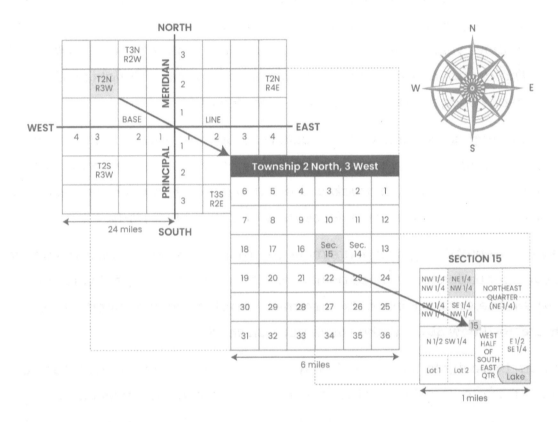

Description: the correct land description for the highlighted property parcel here above would be indicated as: "NE1/NW1/4, Sec. 15, T2N, R3W"

(means: Northeast quarter of the northwest quarter of Section nr. 15 of Township 2 North, Range 3 West)

5 - Mineral, Air, and Water Rights!

Every property comes along with certain rights. The three most common rights can help add more value to the property, especially if it's agricultural land.

These are:

- **Mineral Rights:** *As the word suggests, having mineral rights for any land or property makes you eligible to mine any mineral resources and sell them. Now, two parties can also be expected in a case when one party owns the surface rights (only what lies above the land) while the other holds the mineral rights.*

- **Air Rights:** *This pertains to rights that are more related to space above the real land or property. For example, if you have air rights, then you can control who flies above your property. This is a plus point to remember especially if you are selling a property to someone who loves privacy. Also, air rights safeguard you from any bridge or building passing over your land.*

- **Water Rights:** *Essentially for agricultural properties, water rights are necessary because they allow one to alter the course of water and use it for irrigation from natural resources, such as lakes, rivers, and ponds. In rare cases, people owning water rights can even sell or lease the water to another party.*

These were a few of the rights that are more common throughout the world. If an investor or a developer understands these points, then it can serve as a great value addition to their experience. Once again, we should remind you of the golden principle in real estate, **"the more you know about it, the easier you can sell it"**.

Apart from these rights, there are often moral obligations so let's quickly see how they work in real estate. Keep in mind that it is very important to know a bit about it.

C. Encumbrances and effects on property ownership

Have you ever heard the word encumbrances elsewhere?

Encumbrances are simply retainable rights that can affect property ownership. It can also be a legal interest by some parties. For example, you buy land somewhere but in your deal, you agreed to some sort of a deal that you won't sell in the next 10 years. Let's just assume that.

Now, every deal is on paper. So, that paper where you agreed to the terms and conditions, is now acting as an encumbrance for you. Because your rights to sell the property are retained for some 10 years (in this imaginative case only).

It can be of many types. But the foremost ones are mentioned below:

- **Usage Restriction:** *As mentioned in the previous example, restrictions on use restrict how a person owns the property. It can either be stopping them from selling it to keeping some land unused because a passage lane was agreed upon there. If it's an ancient or cultural property, then it can also come with a restriction of building certain structures around or on the property.*

- **Liens:** *A better way to call this would be a financial obligation. For example, your selling rights are restricted because you hold a mortgage or debt against it, that you have to pay to someone to retain those rights.*

- **Easements:** *These are simply legal rights that allow someone else to use your property for a specific purpose. Just like where you agreed on a passageway from your land. With easement rights, utility companies that look after the infrastructure can use it for a specific purpose like spreading a pipeline or installing poles.*

- **Licenses:** *Now, a passageway can be there forever. But if you were only looking to give someone legal rights but for a temporary period, what would you do? You will sign the license which will act as permission so that they can use your land or property for whatever purpose you have agreed upon.*

- **Encroachments:** *Imagine you built a building and you are very happy with it until someone comes and claims you destroyed one of its walls because it used a slight portion of their land as well. You have encroached on someone else's land. Now this is very common as it can occur due to slight miscalculations, inaccurate property surveys or descriptions, and so on. Encroachments can often result in legal disputes which should be solved through mutual agreement or any court proceedings or by signing some easements to remediate the situation.*

- **Defects in Titles:** *Sometimes, the title status of a property is defective because of mistakes in paper records, undisclosed easements or encroachments, or any disputes related to the property. This results in properties with a dispute in titles.*

These were some of the most common types of encumbrances that can affect the value of any property. It is advisable that before closing a deal, you should ask your clients (buyer or seller) to share whether they have any encumbrances or not. This will only ease your work in the future, plus would serve a good purpose for your reputation.

D. Types of Ownership

Since we discussed in the previous section that properties can come with certain legal rights retained, it also affects the status of ownership (properties with no dispute status on title).

There are several forms in which a property can be owned. Below mentioned are a few of them:

- **Tenants in Common:** *Imagine a property is owned by two people (co-owners) and both of them hold a 50% share in it. In this kind of ownership, one owner can sell their share (50% in this case) without the consent of the other partner. And if one of them dies, their share will be passed to an heir rather than the other partner. Note that, it can be owned by two or more people.*

- **Joint Tenants:** *This is also a form of co-ownership where two or more partners own a property but unlike Tenants in Common, this comes with a survivorship. If one of the partners dies, their share is automatically passed to the surviving partner instead of being passed to an heir. Typically, joint tenancy requires unity of title, time, possession, and interest.*

- **Sole Ownership:** *As the term implies, this relates to the complete ownership of a property by a sole person. All of the rights are held by the owning party and can also include water, mineral, and air rights. This form of ownership is common for residential and business-*related properties.

1 - Common Interest Ownership

Similar to the ownerships we previously discussed, common-interest ownership occurs when different parties come together to buy and own a property. Where multiple individuals shared a joint interest in the development of a property. Now, since we can have different case scenarios in a common-interest ownership, let's discuss a few popular ones.

1. **Timeshares:** *In this type of common interest ownership, multiple partners sign an agreement where they wish to use (typically a resort at a tourist attraction or an apartment) for a specified period each year. For example, an apartment is co-owned and time shared by three partners. Each of them uses the property for four months. Now, this depends on the agreement to which the co-owning party comes.*

2. **Condominiums:** *As it sounds, condominiums are a type of common interest ownership in which multiple partners own condos within a building and are often subjected to maintain and look after the part that they own, with a possibility of an extension in management responsibilities for areas such as hallways, and staircases, and swimming pools. For example, an office can be divided into 4 condos with each condo owned by a sole owner. And they have designated management responsibilities to each other.*

3. **Co-ops:** Just like a company gets incorporated, the same works for properties as well. Co-ops (housing cooperatives) are a type of ownership in which multiple owners instead of owning their share, collectively, own and operate a multi-unit property. They together form the cooperative corporation which collectively runs and maintains it. Just like the board members of a company, they are responsible for who becomes the resident and how the mortgage, property taxes, operating expenses, and other liabilities will be managed!

2 - Ownership is severalty/sole ownership

This is perhaps the most common ownership type, especially when it comes to residential properties. As it sounds, it simply means that a property or an estate is owned and run by a single person, a sole owner.

The sole owner is responsible for mortgage payments, liabilities, and property taxes, and decides who can come into the property (as tenants or as buyers). Thus exercising full control over the property. The sole owner is also responsible for managing and planning the estate for future developments.

Since we have a sole owner in this type of ownership, all of the liabilities that come with the estate are to be dealt with by him/her. This can include any debt, social obligations, and other liabilities that have been agreed upon and signed by the owner. No third party can mitigate the situation.

These are some pros and cons of owning a property solely. But you can always imagine and put yourself in touch with real estate situations. Imagine that you are the sole owner, what moral, social, or financial obligations do you expect?

Once a few thoughts start coming to your head, note them down. These are your case scenarios and just by doing this 5-minute imaginative exercise, you are now able to deal with 80% of client inquiries and disputes that might be coming ahead in your real estate journey.

Trust us, it's that simple. Now, let's wrap up this chapter by taking a sneak peek into our last topic.

3 - Life Estate Ownership

Life estate ownership is perhaps the most wonderful type of ownership that you will experience when you start your professional career. It is leaning more towards the heritage or philanthropic side. We will explain that in a while.

In life estate ownership, an individual allows a person (which can be themselves) that we can call a life tenant to use the property for a lifetime. This lifetime period of a life tenant is called "measuring life".

They can occupy it as per their will. However, in this case, a remainder man is appointed. It's simply a person who gets the ownership of the property when the measuring life runs out. It runs out only when the life tenant dies or agrees to end the life estate contract.

Now, there are some aspects that you need to keep in mind:

- Life tenants get to enjoy the lifetime usage of a property. They exercise the same rights as if they were the complete ownership of the property (except for a few cases mentioned next).

- In this case, life estate ownership is knotted with measuring life. If Josh's parents grant a life estate to him, then his parent's life is the measuring life here. And when that runs out, Josh (as the remainder man here) will be the complete owner of the property. Thus comes the heritage. The same goes for charities. For example, a notable businessman signs a life estate for a charity and when he dies, the charity gets all of the properties.

- When the life estate is terminated, the remainder man has a legal claim to the property. That's why in case you want to sell your life estate property, you will need the consent of the remainder man to do so. Otherwise, you can't sell a life estate.

In the end, life estate ownership mostly occurs when heirs in a family are nominated. It can be a specific individual as well. Note that, with a life estate, property taxes might behave differently for different case scenarios. So, search your local (whichever territory you are in) catalog of taxes, or consult a professional when you have started your career after passing your exam.

Exercise Questions

1. *A rectangular piece of land measures 300 feet by 500 feet. What is the total area of the land in acres?*

Use the formula:

Total Area (in acres) = Length (ft) x Width (ft) / 43,560

2. A residential property has a livable area of 1,800 square feet, but the total rentable area is 2,200 square feet. What is the percentage of unusable space in the property?

Use the formula:

Unusable Space (%) = (1 – livable area/rentable area) x 100%

3. If a homeowner grants another person the right to live in their house for the duration of their lifetime, what type of ownership arrangement is this?

Chapter 2

LAND USE CONTROLS & REGULATIONS

In the world of real estate and properties today, everything works in a certain order, one which is maintained by the government and state and its various institutions. A better way to express it would be that it is regulated.

As a real estate agent, it is your dire duty to understand how regulations and land usage work on different levels of government. And as we have always followed our motto, "the more we know, the better the outcome", the same applies to this.

We would not hesitate to call it the knowledge that sets a real estate agent apart from 50% of people in this professional space. If we know the regulations, then we know how to settle our client's disputes or any potential cases. It is similar to expanding your options when you start (after passing your PSI exam of course) so there is more room for success.

So what are these land use controls?

As it appears, it involves the employment of different ordinances and laws to help regulate, run, and conserve the land. It is a very important aspect to be considered, especially by governments because it entails policy making directly. Take this as when the population grows, the usage of land increases, and thus the city expands. Now, with inadequate planning, problems can appear robustly, and we also need to conserve some historic properties, plus a multitude of things, and for each of them, there is a separate law, one that is maintained by various state bodies.

Usually, these land usage controls and regulations are enacted to achieve the following:

- To protect public health and provide safety

- To promote a culture of orderly development within a city or a state

- To ensure that natural resources such as parks, and forests, are preserved

- To improve the quality of life within a neighborhood

Sometimes, there can be several disputes concerning land use controls and regulations. Imagine you live in a neighborhood and suddenly there is a bridge built around where you live. Now, the traffic is fast and there is often noise. Because of that, your property is now devalued.

So, who's responsible for this? The 14th Amendment gives you multiple rights. And that's why you would want to be compensated. Right when you decide it, the question of "how" pops up.

That "**how**" is what we study in land use controls and regulations. That's why at the start, we mentioned its importance. There are a few chapters in this book that you will have to work more on when you have started your career. This is one of them.

Let's now take a brief look at how government rights in land works. And then we will delve deeper into how the government regulates the overall land, in line with the government's policy.

A. Government Rights In Land

As it sounds (we keep repeating it so you remember the whole section and so you can recall it by just focusing on the sound of the word and the meaning it conveys), the government has several rights, powers, and interests that directly relate with key property factors like its ownership and usage.

Let's take a look at them one by one.

1 - Property Taxes & Assessments

Property taxes are imposed by governments based on the actual value of a property. This value depends on the assessment by a professional or state agent. Now, every property owner, as you might already know, has to submit their taxes annually. Not doing so, and they will be bound by foreclosures and some penalties.

Apart from the general assessment of land, there are some additional charges or penalties that can be imposed. We call them special assessments and their sole purpose is to finance public improvements or, in some cases, it can also be for the overall benefit of the property. This can range from road repairs, and building sidewalks to some utility upgrades.

As we discussed earlier, this is for the overall improvement of property owners so they get the maximum benefit from the project.

2 - Eminent Domain, Escheat, and Condemnation

When a government takes private property for anything related to public use and provides you with fair compensation, then that's **Eminent Domain**. This right has been given to the governments in the 5th Amendment of the U.S. Constitution. According to the 5th Amendment, governments can't take private property without providing a "just" compensation to the owner.

Also, it is the duty of the government to issue you an earlier notice followed by some appraisals until they offer you a fair price. As mentioned earlier, it can be for anything related to public use, from constructing roads to building a bridge, or maybe a sidewalk.

Imagine a land owner passes away and the state cannot locate any of the heirs or beneficiaries, what happens to the land? The government acquires it to be used for public use. **Escheat** is a process in which a government acquires unclaimed land (after continuous failed attempts in searching for any heir or beneficiaries) by exercising its eminent domain powers that allow it to take private property (with a just compensation) and use it for public use.

Note that, escheat laws are for both real property as well as personal one. Also, a state has various procedures and protocols for identifying and acquiring properties.

In the end, the legal process by which the government exercises its powers derived from eminent domain is called **condemnation**. Ideally, this process can contain the following steps:

- **Action by the Government:** *when the government declares its intent to take private property*

- **Issuance of Notice to Property Owners:** *When decided the government issues a notice explaining their interest in the property, and the proposed project, while also detailing the owners about the rights that they hold in the whole condemnation process.*

- **Negotiations:** *It is when talks take place between the government and property owners. Various matters such as the pricing of the property, its fair value and compensation, and related affairs are discussed.*

- **Appraisals:** *Now, if the owner has high demands and negotiations fail, then the government resorts to its next action, conducting a fair market valuation of the property, which is a price at which both selling and buying parties agree without distress.*

- **The Legal Battle:** *Even if still the negotiations fail and an agreement cannot be reached then the government initiates the condemnation process filing a lawsuit. Now, the government has a right to take private property with just compensation as laid out in the 5th Amendment.*

- *After that, court proceedings commence, with each party (the government and property owner) providing their pieces of evidence for a fair market evaluation, upon which the jury decides and sets the "just compensation".*

- **Payment and Transferring of Title:** *After that, payments are made to the property owner the title is transferred to the government, and the project for public use starts.*

Now that we know enough about government rights in land, we also need to take a look at how the government exercises its control. So, let's move forward and see how things work around this side of the real estate world.

B. Government Controls

To promote the welfare of society, provide them with a safe neighborhood, and facilities, and regulate land expansion, the government exercises various controls for different cases which will be mentioned right after we discuss what police powers are:

"The power of government (mostly at a local level) to promote laws influenced at the overall welfare of the society, their safety, and rights. All of this to regulate and promote property rights, land use, and its expansion."

Let's now see the various expressions in which these government controls take place in line with when police powers are expected.

1 - Zoning and Master Plans

To promote stable land usage and development within its jurisdiction, a local government ensures that everything is kept and constructed as per the zoning guidelines. Usually, land is divided into different zones and districts which are further divided into sub-zones such as residential and commercial zones. As you might have guessed, the duty of the government here is to exercise its police power to ensure that land usage and development ensures the quality of life which is the basic right of every citizen. That's what we can call **zoning**, and the laws will be referred to as zoning laws.

Now all of the zoning laws depend directly on a **master plan**. A master plan contains a framework or a future map explaining how infrastructure will be maintained and designed over the coming years, where the residents will settle, how will commercial zones expand, how transport will be managed, and how all of this respects the environmental conservation laws. These laws are also influenced by the zoning laws and long-term land usage policies, all of which ensure stable growth in a society, city, or even a state (when multiple master plans and zoning decisions work in perfect harmony with the overall policy and regulations of the state).

2 - Building Codes

The minimum standards for renovating, maintaining, or constructing buildings are set by the government (local and state) with a policy focus on ensuring the overall quality of life, rights being delivered, and welfare of the society. These minimum standards are called building codes. They can contain various concerns like:

- Fire safety of the buildings (whether it is designed with enough fire safety measures or not)

- Electrical safety

- Energy efficiency

- The integrity of the structure (does it come with a solid foundation and a stable design?)

All of these factors among many others are to be considered by property owners, real estate developers, and people who are involved in the construction. The police power here acts in the form of routine inspections or reviews of permits to make sure that everything is in line with the set regulations and standards. It's for the safety of the public.

3 - Regulation of Special Land Types

Oftentimes, a land can be situated in areas where environmental hazards are imminent. Therefore, for better promotion of rights, there are some special regulations for these land types:

a. **Flood Zones:** *Sometimes, land is located in any of the flood zones (areas where there is a higher chance of a flood). These areas are designated by the Federal Emergency Management Authority (FEMA) based on their data for assessing flood risk. Now, flood zones can be subjected to various regulations such as:*

- *Regulations that demand the usage of flood-friendly material (one that resists floods)*

- *Restrictions on new constructions*

- *Building techniques and designs that promote flood safety*

- *In some cases, each property owner has to get flood insurance*

- *All of these regulations are to promote the safety of the people when floods finally arrive.*

b. **Wet Lands:** *Sometimes land can be situated in areas that are sensitive environmentally. Property owners are often regulated to protect degrading ecosystems or wildlife. Also, projects that fall near the wetlands and that can affect any wetlands are subjected to wetlands mitigation laws as well. Normally, wetlands areas are ones:*

- *Having environmental significance (an area where endangered habitats are located)*

- *Having a natural tendency to protect the population from floods and strong winds*

- *Having a key role in improving the water quality which might be used by the people.*

4 - Regulation of Environmental Hazards

In certain cases, there are several potential hazards that can affect the overall stature of public safety and health standards. Therefore, it is important for us to understand its types and how regulation works for those types.

a. **Types of Hazards:** We live in a world full of chemicals. With each chemical, especially in the construction and development process, comes a potential environmental hazard that has to be taken care of (that's why it is regulated). These hazards directly or indirectly affect the health of people and damage the environment. It can include:

- Usage of lead-based paints

- Hazardous waste

- Asbestos, a mineral occurring in rocks or soil which is microscopic-level. Inhaling these fibers can bolster the risk of immense health issues such as asbestosis, mesothelioma, or even, lung cancer

- Mold and radon gas

That's the reason it is regulated so the property owners, tenants, or collectively, communities are safe from these environmental hazards.

b. **Abatement & Mitigation:** *Abatement refers to the removal or containment of potentially hazardous substances to reduce the risk of diseases or further expansion. While, on the other hand, mitigation refers to the overall deployment of policies and regulations to lower the impact of any environmental hazard.*

This can often require property owners to maintain their ventilation systems, seal off any contaminated material (professionals should be contacted in this concern for their safety), and remediation. The owners are often required to have routine abatement and mitigation inspections to make sure that their and public safety is maintained.

c. **Restrictions on contaminated property:** *Oftentimes, a property can be subjected to restriction on use, development, or even transferring of title, to ensure that public health and safety standards are up to the mark. If a party is affected by any environmental hazard, then the respective property owner can also face legal battles, a devaluation in price, and legal penalties for the cleanup of environmentally hazardous substances.*

C. Private controls

Up till now, we have seen government controls and regulations. In real estate, there are some private controls as well. These regulations are imposed by private owners developers or homeowner associations (HOAs) and are related to maintaining, using, or developing real property.

Now, private controls can be of the following types:

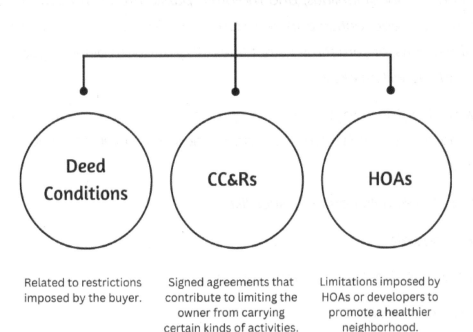

Private Controls

Deed Conditions
Related to restrictions imposed by the buyer.

CC&Rs
Signed agreements that contribute to limiting the owner from carrying certain kinds of activities.

HOAs
Limitations imposed by HOAs or developers to promote a healthier neighborhood.

1. ***Deed Conditions or Restrictions:*** *Sometimes a few restrictions can be imposed by the property owner regarding the possible usage, building standards or design, or some other conditions that are duly signed when a transfer is being made. The owner can have different motives behind their conditions but most of them are because of maintaining the aesthetics of the neighborhood or even protecting the value of property.*

   It is important to note here that any deed conditions or restrictions imposed on land or property will run for the rest of its life (forever) and in case of violations, strict legal action can be taken against the violator of the deed conditions (by any affected party, organization, or person who issued the restrictions).

2. ***Covenant, Conditions, and Restrictions (CC&Rs):*** *These are signed agreements (mostly contracts) that reserve the property owner their usage of the land in specific ways, and require the following of certain rules, as demanded by the party issuing the CC&Rs, which is mostly developers and builders.*

These are often issued to find mutual consent to help regulate the usage of property, protect community guidelines, and maintain public areas. In case of violations of these contracts, legal action can be taken by the issuing party, which can result in serious limitations, or sometimes strict fines. It's just about being a good member of society and you will be okay.

That's why all of these regulations (the previous ones as well) are so important to understand as they just widen your imagination, which will help you immensely in your exam.

In the end, CC&Rs help cater to issues like:

- *Regulating pets*

- *Traffic and parking rules within a society*

- *Noise level restrictions*

- *Usage and guidelines for common areas (public)*

- *Architectural guidelines such as the design and size of the building as well as the material usage.*

3. ***Homeowners Associations (HOAs):*** *As it sounds, HOAs are limitations and regulations imposed by homeowner associations or developers of a confined community. All of these regulations are to cater to issues that were mentioned right in the previous section (CC&Rs). Just like before, violation of HOAs can result in limitation in the use of property or fines or legal penalties.*

All of these factors that were discussed in this chapter detailed more about how controls occur on governmental and private levels and what are the factors that you can expect when you start your professional career. It is advisable here to always seek a legal professional for assistance in legal issues. If you have this in your skillset, you will set quite a remarkable example for people who follow you. Also, this is an important section of your exam so in case you have to read it twice, don't hesitate.

Exercise Questions

1. You own a property assessed at $300,000, and the tax rate in your area is 1.5%. Calculate the annual property tax you owe.

    Use the formula:

    Property Tax = Property Assessment Value × Tax Rate

2. You are planning to open a small retail store in a residential area. Explain how zoning laws might affect your business and what steps you can take to comply with them?

3. You are considering purchasing a property located near a former industrial site. Explain the potential environmental hazards associated with such properties and what measures can be taken to mitigate these risks?

Chapter 3

VALUATION & MARKET ANALYSIS

Perhaps the most dynamic aspect of real estate is valuation and market analysis. It is important to understand the fundamentals of this aspect because you will find them everywhere. Because price is everywhere and it is so important. Without it, no buying and selling can occur, and in the case of refinancing mortgages, it is very important to understand these factors.

Now, valuation is related to the process by which a property is valued.

Market analysis, as it sounds, is the process by which we analyze a real estate market based on different factors and economic indicators. Now, a market analysis of any market is not limited, and thus, depends on one's wish to research as much as one can.

Let's take a quick look at all the important factors that are related to valuation and market analysis. The first on our list is "appraisals".

A. Appraisals

If a purchase of a property has to be made, it is important to determine its exact value. The process that helps us achieve that motive is called appraisals, the fair value of a property. This process can include considerations like the condition of a property (in case a structure is built), the location, the age of the construction, the number of rooms and bathrooms, the aesthetic appeal, the design, and whether it comes with a garden that has rare flowers in it.

Now, appraisals are what both parties (buyer and seller) agree on. Let's take a deeper look at appraisals:

1. **Purpose and use of appraisals for valuation:** *Our end goal with appraisals is to find an unbiased and legitimate price of a property to help facilitate the transfer process or any other purposes. As mentioned earlier, this can involve assessing the overall market demographics, data that indicates sales at a local or national level, the type and features of the property, or the general benefits that come with it.*

   Normally, appraisals facilitate purposes like:

   - *Financing or refinancing (when mortgage payments are revised based on late interest rates and monetary policy) of mortgages*

   - *Sale transactions*

   - *Insurance (to set rates and payments)*

   - *Planning of an estate*

   - *Taxation (the most important reason)*

2. **General steps in the appraisal process:** *Before we explain all the important steps of the appraisal process, note that these valuations are often done by certified appraisers to get an actual and accurate value of a property.*

   This process typically includes:

   a. **Finding the intent/purpose of the appraisal:** *In this process, the purpose of an appraisal is determined. It can be any from the list mentioned in the previous section. Keep in mind that this information is important for the appraiser because different purposes require different approaches.*

   b. **Gathering Property Information:** *In this step, the appraiser gathers essential information such as age, location, size, design, layout of the property, any recent installments, or characteristics that add more to the value of the property.*

   c. **Inspection:** *In this step, the appraiser visits the property for a detailed assessment which is based on the initial information he collected about the* property. The appraiser tends to find any defects or issues which can ultimately affect the value of the property and vice versa.

d. **Examining Market Data:** *In this step, the appraiser researches different sets of data such as MLS (multiple listing services), sales and property records, fluctuations in prices in relevance with increased inflation, or other sets of data that can help assess the market value of a property.*

e. **Finding a comparative property:** *Once everything is examined, the appraiser might opt for finding a property that is similar to the one he/she is examining to find out how the other one is priced. The comparative data helps the appraiser in reaching a fair price. In the same way, the appraiser might examine comparable sales data as well.*

f. **Market Value Adjustments:** *In this step, the appraiser makes certain adjustments and employs professional appraisal methods. These value adjustments are based on comparable sales and market data.*

g. **A final reconciliation by the appraiser:** *Once all measures have been made, the appraiser revises the whole process by inspecting different appraisal approaches that were employed and which according to their knowledge and experience is the certified value of a property.*

h. **Preparing the Appraisal Report:** *In the final step, a report is prepared by the appraiser indicating the analysis opted for appraisal, the findings (based on comparable data and appraisal techniques/methods), and a final opinion about the fair value of the property.*

3. **Situations requiring appraisals by a certified appraiser:** *Now that we know about the general appraisal process, these are some of the situations that can require you to hire a certified appraiser:*

a. **Transactions:** *For a sale or purchase to occur, an appraisal can be required. But in case one is planning to fund the purchase with a loan, then the lender will require an appraisal by a certified appraiser.*

b. **Mortgage Financing & Refinancing:** *As mentioned previously, this can be required by the lender when mortgage rates and duration are being settled.*

c. **HELOCs:** *An appraisal by a certified appraiser is required in case of home equity loans or line of credits (HELOCs) to find the value of available equity in case one is planning to borrow a loan.*

d. **Property Tax Assessment:** *It is often required by the governments as one can expect.*

e. **For eminent domain and escheat proceedings**

f. **For insurance and divorce settlements**

g. **Settlement of disputes:** *In case a legal battle is going on, the first thing that a court would order is to get an appraisal by a certified appraiser. Without it, the proceedings and disputes cannot be solved.*

B. Estimating Value

In the previous section, we took a look at how the value of a property is determined by the certified appraiser. Not every time we will need to contact a professional for estimation of property's value. Also, you need to understand the basic aspects that you can take for yourself to understand the value of a property better.

Let's take a look at some key aspects that you might want to consider in your assessments:

1. **Effects of economic principles and property characteristics:** *The economic principles and correct evaluation of property characteristics is a real estate agent's most vital feature. This can bolster correct investment decisions along with accurate valuations. These are some of the factors that you might want to consider during this process:*

   a. **Supply and Demand:** *This is perhaps the most basic yet most important factor that tells us about a fair price of any asset, not limited to the real estate market* *only. If the supply is high and demand is low, the price of an asset moves down. If the supply is low and demand is high, the price moves up. Now, while doing this analysis, you can explore population forecasts (the easiest way to predict demand in the future), general employment data and future trends, and the overall trajectory of the economy.*

b. **Location:** *Properties situated in urban centers and schools can be priced higher than those that are away from these centers. It is because the former provides better economic opportunities. Similarly, a property that is in an environmental hazard zone or bad law situation would be less in price. Location is very important when considering any valuations.*

c. **Property Characteristics:** *What does the property look like? What is its age, design, and its pros and cons?*

2. **Sales or Market Comparison Approach:** *As mentioned before it is an important step to consider when valuing a property as an appraiser, sales and market comparison can help support the valuation of a property immensely. These are some of the factors that you might want to consider in this process:*

a. **Finding and Selecting Comparable:** *In this step, we find and select properties that are similar to the property we are valuing. We consider aspects like similar size, dimensions, design, and layout, and in some cases, similar location.*

b. **Market Trends and Conditions:** *In this step, we find comparable sales and market data to understand the holistic market trends over the past years (depending on how far you jump back into the past in terms of data) to gather a vivid perspective of trends and conditions in the market, as well as for the future.*

3. **Cost Approach:** *In certain cases, we can occur upon properties with limited sales data or with unique importance, therefore, we need to employ updated approaches to determine its true value. In this method, a property value is based on the reproducing cost or cost of replacing it with a similar one.*

Now, let's take a look at how these two costs differ and some other aspects that you can consider when following the cost approach:

a. **Reproduction vs Replacement Costs:** *The cost of reproducing a replica of a property is known as reproduction cost. On the other hand, replacement cost is the amount required in constructing a building similar to the one we are assessing, with similar utility and characteristics.*

b. **Depreciation:** *Another important point to consider in this approach is depreciation which means the total loss in value resulting from physical wear and tear of the property or any obsolescence.*

c. **Land Value & Improvements:** *The value of a property depends both on land and any construction on it. To find a fair value of a property, you might want to examine the fair value of land by using comparable data, while also researching the market for the cost of improvements. This will help determine the total value (land + improvements) of a property which will further facilitate the negotiations round or any court proceedings.*

d. **General Market Conditions:** *You might also want to conduct a general survey of the market, finding the latest prices for building materials, or checking the availability of labor and their estimated cost, in case you were to hire them. You might also want to check the building code requirements so you don't have to deal with any potential penalties or fines.*

4. **Income Analysis Approach:** *In certain cases, one might want to value a property that generates an income, mostly in terms of rental. For these kinds of properties such as offices, apartments, commercial shops, and so on, you might want to follow the following aspects to find a fair value of these properties:*

a. **Rental Income & Cash Flow:** *In this income approach, we examine factors like the total rental income of the property, operating and maintenance expenses, and net operating income (NOI) which can be obtained by subtracting operating* *expenses from the total income of the property. This helps us to identify the overall cash flow (to be expected as well) and rental income of the property.*

b. **Using Capitalization Rates:** *Also known as cap rates, these represent the average return that investors get/expect on their investments (in the real estate sector). This can depend on a multitude of factors such as location and factors that we keep repeating here. Ultimately, these cap rates help turn the NOI into an estimated value. Keep in mind that this technique is mostly opted by the appraisers but in some cases, investors have their approaches to do so.*

Factors like these help agents, appraisers, or investors to find the potential of a property both in terms of income and cash flow which further contributes to a fair valuation of a property. All of these aspects have capacitated you with a fair understanding of how valuation and different market analysis techniques work. Keep in mind that this depends on the amount of effort one is putting in. Especially in the case of market analysis, there is no limit to what you can do, such as one might be reading and checking the news, the FED rates, inflation, or potential bubbles in an economy. It all depends on the motive of the beholder.

That being said, we are confident enough that this will help you get through your exam. Now, let's move on to another topic that you need to know about, it is a very important chapter for the PSI National Real Estate exam!

5. **GRM & GIM:** *In real estate, there are certain income-generating properties. In order to evaluate their performance and the expected return it can produce we use these two metrics:*

   a. **Gross Rent Multiplier:** *GRM is a ratio that helps calculate the potential return on investment. It is the ratio of the purchase price of a property and gross annual rental income as shown in the formula:*

   GRM = Purchase Price / Annual Rental Income

   For example, there is a property that generates $50,000 in annual rental income, and its seller is asking $500,000 for it. The GRM, in this case, would be:

GRM = $500,000 / $50,000

GRM = 10

It means that for every 10 dollars invested in this property will yield 1 dollar in rental income for you. It is a return of 10% (a good one).

b. **Gross Income Multiplier:** *Sometimes a property can bolster income apart from rental income. It can be a bonus income or a sudden hike in prices because of high demand. We use the same formula, but when using this method, we take into account the gross income of the property including rental income:*

GIM = Purchase Price / Total Annual Income

Note that, in GRM & GIM, a return after taxes and fees of 10% is remarkable, while anything above it is beyond exceptional. You are getting the same return as if you were getting in an average stock market year.

Now, we have a few questions for you to solve:

1. A property generates $150,000 in gross annual rental income and is priced at $1,200,000. Calculate its GRM.

2. Another property generates $150,000 in gross annual income and is priced at $2,250,000. Calculate its GIM.

3. If the GRM of a property is 8 and its gross annual rental income is $80,000, what is its purchase price?

4. A property has a GIM of 12 and its gross annual income is $180,000. What is its purchase price?

Chapter 4

FINANCING

Financing in real estate simply means the methods and ways by which an investor can secure financing for their properties. Sometimes we have cash and sometimes we don't have it. There are numerous options available to investors or people willing to start a career out of the real estate industry.

There are two things to keep in mind when financing real estate ventures:

✓ *What works for everyone might not work for you so one needs to research the best possible financing options for themselves.*

✓ *There is nothing wrong with opting for financing options because it increases your cash flow, thus favoring your investment options.*

A. Basic Concepts and Terminologies

For a better understanding, let's see what are the basic concepts that you need to know in order to understand and get the maximum out of financing options. Also, it is a very important chapter in reference to your real estate exam so don't hesitate to read it over and again in case you are unable to understand it the first time:

1. **Points:** These refer to the one-time payment that you will have to pay to your lender upfront so that when your monthly mortgage or installment for loan return is being calculated, the number is comfortable for you to return or pay back. Typically, one point means 1% of upfront payments (of the total loan). If you pay 10 points upfront, then you will have a lower monthly mortgage payment than if you were to pay 5 points, thus reducing your interest rate.

Answer this question for us please (solution in chapter 12):

"You are considering taking out a mortgage for $300,000 to purchase a property. The lender offers you two options:

Option A: Pay 3 points upfront, reducing your interest rate to 4.5%.

Option B: Pay 5 points upfront, reducing your interest rate to 4.0%.

Calculate the upfront payment for each option and determine which option would result in a lower monthly mortgage payment."

2. **Loan to Value Ratio (LTV):** It's a simple metric that is often used by lenders. It is a ratio of the loan amount divided by the property's value or purchase price (which is in percentage). A lower LTV ratio is what every lender is looking for because it constitutes a lower risk for the lender. If the LTV ratio is higher, then it means that borrower has a higher chance of defaulting on their payments. The LTV ratio is typically used for PMI.

3. **Private Mortgage Insurance (PMI):** It's a designed insurance method to protect the lender in case their borrower default or is unable to pay back the requested loan amount in a given time. Mostly, when the borrower's down payment is less than 20% (20 points), then the lender might want him/her to get a PMI which will continue until the borrower's LTV ratio has reached a safe threshold.

In case, you are opting for PMI, you need to keep in mind that you will have to pay an additional amount along with your monthly mortgage payments. When the LTV ratio is safe, you can cancel your PMI plan only when your lender agrees to it.

4. **Interest:** It is simply what borrowing money from the lender costs you. If you are borrowing $100,000 at a 10% interest rate, then the total amount that you will return will be $110,000. It is important to opt only for annual interest instead of monthly interest which will deteriorate your whole financial stature. There are two types of interest:

- **Fixed Interest Rate**: which remains fixed throughout the life of a contract.

- **Adjustable Interest Rate**: which fluctuates about market conditions, inflation, and policy changes (FED and related institutions)

Its formula is:

Interest = (Loan Amount) x (Interest Rate) x (Loan Term in years or months)

Using the formula, try to solve this problem:

You're comparing two mortgage options for a property purchase: one with a fixed interest rate and another with an adjustable interest rate. The property costs **$500,000**.

The fixed-rate mortgage offers an interest rate of **3.8%** for **20** years, while the adjustable-rate mortgage starts at 3.5% for the first 5 years, and then adjusts annually based on market conditions. Assuming the adjustable-rate mortgage adjusts by 0.25% annually after the initial 5-year period, calculate the total interest paid over 20 years for both options.

For the adjustable-rate mortgage:

Average Interest Rate = (Initial Interest Rate + Final Interest Rate) / 2

After calculating the total interest paid for both options, compare them to determine which mortgage is more cost-effective over the long term.

5. **PITI:** It might sound complex but it is really simple. PITI stands for Principal, Interest, Taxes, and Insurance. Together, these four sum your total mortgage payments. The principal amount refers to the amount to be paid excluding any interest rates (the actual borrowed amount). We have discussed interest rates just before. Taxes are often imposed by local government (seek a financial advisor when doing so) and Insurance helps you to protect your property against any sort of damages or disasters.

Usually, money lenders like to see the PITI to be less than or equal to 28% of the borrower's total income (source: Investopedia) but this can vary from lender to lender as they too need to be competitive in their industry.

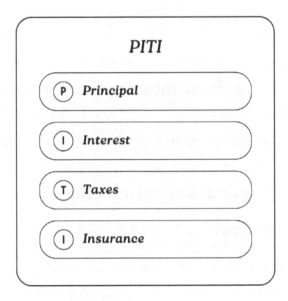

6. **Financing Instruments:** It means an instrument through which you can finance your real estate goals. We have taken a good look at what is required generally from the lender side and some basic concepts. Let's see a couple more and then we will specify which types of loans exist and some topics related to general credit:

- A mortgage is simply an agreement between lender and borrower pertaining to financing investments in real estate. We have already discussed that you don't need a lot of capital to start investing in real estate, opting for financial instruments is another good choice. In a mortgage, the property you are buying is typically kept as collateral in case you are unable to abide by your mortgage agreement, and the borrower is required to pay monthly payments (in most cases) that are calculated on the basis of principal and interest rates.

- A promissory note is simply a promise or an agreement that will act as a piece of evidence between a borrower and a lender for the repayment of money with agreed interest rates. It can include terms and conditions imposed by the lender, fines and penalties in case there are violations of the agreement, amount to be paid by the borrower, agreed interest rate, etc.

B. Types of Loans

Now that we have discussed the general terminologies that are used in real estate financing, it is time for us to specify our knowledge and take a sneak peek into the types of loans that usually exist all around the world. Once again, we should remind you not all options work the same for everyone and that's why you need to know more about different kinds of loans so that you can help your clients or even yourself when you start your career in this world of opportunities and real estate.

These are some of the basic types:

1. **Conventional Loans:** These loans are not backed by any government. Instead, they are conventional in nature, meaning that these are provided by private lenders, usually credit unions or banks. Keep in mind, that, unlike government-backed loans, you might need a really good credit rating, and you might be required to pay a healthy down payment to acquire them. Also, since it is private, the interest rates can be variable, and you might have to face stricter requirements.

2. **FHA Insured Loans:** These are government-backed loans provided by the Federal Housing Authority (FHA) which is a government institution or agency. FHA-insured loans don't require strict guidelines and one can secure these loans even with a marginal credit rating and a low down payment. But to provide security to the lenders, these loans are typically associated with MIPs (mortgage insurance premiums) which can add to your total mortgage cost. Overall, it is a good financing option.

3. **VA Guaranteed Loans:** If you are a military veteran, an active military personnel, or even a spouse of a military personal (deceased), you can qualify for this lucrative loan. It's because you don't need to pay any down payment, you get competitive interest rates, and you don't need to bear the extra burden of MIPs. These loans are provided by the Department of Veteran Affairs (VA).

4. **USDA/Rural Loan Program:** As it sounds, these loans are meant for homebuyers living in rural areas. These loans are administered by the United States Department of Agriculture and offer low or zero down payments. Also, if you qualify for these loans, you will get competitive interest rates. Keep in mind that not all rural areas qualify for these loans and there can be certain income thresholds required for these.

5. **Amortized Loans:** Imagine you are looking to get a loan; wouldn't you want to get a detailed overview of your monthly payments for the rest of your loan tenure? Amortized loans help you in this regard. In these types of loans, your payment is scheduled, with more focus on paying the interest rate first and once you have paid it, in the end, you will just need to pay back the principal amount. A common example of amortized loans is fixed-rate mortgages, with interest rates remaining the same for the rest of the loan period.

6. **Adjustable-Rate Mortgages (ARMs):** It's the exact opposite of amortized loans or fixed-rate mortgages. In ARMs, the interest rate is variable depending on a multitude of factors like government policy, market conditions, fluctuations, and sometimes, even competition in markets. Just a quick fact, ARMs usually offer lower interest rates in the beginning so that these are attractive for buyers, as they will have to pay low monthly payments. But you must be prepared for an adjustment in the interest rate, in the near future, which can lead to potentially higher monthly payments. Therefore, a buyer should seek only this when they understand all of the terms very well, plus, they have a good overview and knowledge about market forecasts and the general economy.

7. **Bridge Loans:** Imagine you are looking for a loan to buy a new real property and you also have another property to sell. Now, it's a good idea if you can use the other property (to be sold) as collateral to get friendly terms on your loan. To do that, bridge loans come to your rescue. It's a temporary solution that bridges property to be sold and the purchase of a newer property. Mostly, people get bridge loans to pay down payments until the buyer has sold the existing property.

Also, people opt for these kinds of loans when they need to make quick arrangements.

8. **Owner Financing:** As it sounds, one can opt for owner financing when they don't want to include the government or any private lending entity in the buying of a property. In this type of financing, the owner acts as a lender while the seller is required to pay agreed installments to the lender (owner). When all of the installments are paid, the transfer of title occurs. Note that, a legal agreement should be signed between buyer and seller to avoid any confusion and disputes in the future.

Now, you know about different types of loans. It is crucial for real estate agents or professionals to understand these types and store them in their memory because they will need them when their clients want to buy a property but they are looking to finance it in some favorable way. Discuss with them all the prospects and requirements and then suggest the most favorable option to your clients. With that being said, let us now move on to discussing the process side of these loans.

C. Financing and Lending – The process

We know about loans and different means of securing financing for real estate endeavors. Now, it is time for us to take a brief sneak peek into the process so that you as a real estate professional can guide your clients in a detailed manner, further escalating your credibility.

1. **Lending Process Application Through Closing:** This is perhaps the most crucial phase in all of the real estate transactions. It's because we can find a number of loan options easily, but for those who do have not a lot of expertise or those who are first-time homebuyers, it can get difficult or confusing at times.

The process starts with the buyer submitting a mortgage application to the lender. This can require the following information:

- **Financial status**

- **Employment history**

- **Previous track record**

- **Any other documents or information** (which varies from lender to lender)

Once it is submitted it is time for the lender to assess the application using their criteria (which are mostly pivoted by their experience) and find out whether the buyer is trustworthy or not. Also, the lender verifies the provided information in the application, and then all they need to find is how creditworthy the applicant (buyer) is. Now, this creditworthiness is based on the following aspects:

- Credit rating

- Debt-to-income ratio (we will discuss this at the end of this section)

- Income status

- Employment status (is it stable or part-time)

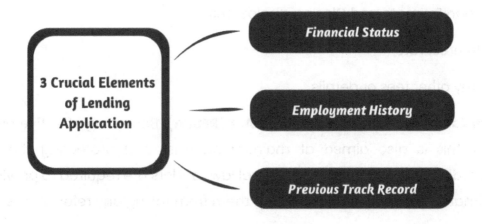

Based on these, any application has to pass the approval process. When it happens, the lender might want to conduct a detailed analysis of the buyer profile, most summing up risks that they can expect with lending to the buyer. Once again, the lender verifies all of the information that is provided to them through different resources. And when everything is up to the mark, the lender provides the buyer with a commitment letter, detailing the terms and conditions of the contract, outlining the agreed interest rate, and payment plan.

In the end, the buyer reviews the contract and then signs it. And that's it, the loan amount is transferred to the buyer's account.

2. **Financing & Credit Law & Rules:** To help regulate the whole lending and financing process, the government has several laws that mitigate the associated risks, and so on. Let's take a brief look at some of the important laws:

   a. **Truth In Lending Act (TILA):** To maintain transparency and protect the borrower, the federal government has imposed this law that requires lenders to share all of the important details and conditions regarding their loan application. This informed use can include the following terms to be stated as "truth", meaning transparency shall be maintained:

      - The contract should outline all of the terms and conditions imposed by the lender without any discrepancies

      - Loan Estimate and Closing disclosures

      - Interest rate

      - Any other fees or details

   b. **Real Estate Settlement Procedure Act (RESPA):** Becoming effective on June 20, 1975, this is also aimed at maintaining trust and protecting the borrower. According to RESPA, which is a federal law, lenders are required to provide honest estimates of closing costs and stop them from taking any referral fees.

   c. **Equal Credit Opportunity Act (ECOA):** As it sounds, this law is aimed at providing fair opportunities to all people. Enacted in 1974, this law maintains the social order and requires lenders to provide loans to people irrespective of color, religion, caste, age, marital status, or nationality. An equal credit opportunity for all!

   d. **CFPB/TRID Rules on Financing & Risky Loan Features:** To help protect consumers, the Consumer Financial Protection Bureau coupled with TRID rules helps promote certain practices aimed at facilitating the borrower and recovering the economy because of the current mortgage crisis. The general rules for risky loan features are:

- For high-cost mortgages, these rules ban huge payments at the end of the loan and penalties in case the borrower returns the loan before the closure timeline.

- It bans any fees to be imposed by the lender when the borrower requests to modify the loan or when they ask for a payoff statement (a document detailing how much the borrower needs to pay off all the remaining loans). Also, it limits consumers to default on their loans so that they can secure a high-rate mortgage once again.

- In the end, these rules require consumers to receive proper guidance and counseling from professionals before seeking a high-risk/rate mortgage.

Now these are some of the general rules that are enacted by the government or institutions to help protect consumers from making riskier decisions and facilitate their loan process. In the lending process, we discussed some terms like debt-to-income ratio so let's take a look at what they are and some other important factors to know about in this financing process.

3. **Underwriting:** It's a very crucial step, especially for lenders, and includes aspects in order to assess the risk associated with lending money to someone. In underwriting, a lender assesses the credit profile and creditworthiness of the borrower based on numerous methods such as:

a. **Debt Ratios:** It's an important metric that helps lenders analyze whether the borrower can manage the debt/financial obligations or not. There are two kinds of debt ratios:

- **Debt-to-Income Ratio (DTI):** As it sounds, in this method, the lender assesses the income of the borrower in relation to the debt that they are seeking.

Though it depends on a down payment or credit score, a rule of thumb is that if it's lower than 43%, then it's safe to lend out money.

This is how you calculate the DTI:

Imagine Josh has a monthly income of $5000 and his monthly debt payments are $1500. His DTI ratio will be:

DTI = (Total Monthly Debt Payments/Total Income) * 100

DTI = (1500/5000) * 100

DTI = 30% (which is favorable and can get the borrower approval)

- **Loan-to-Value Ratio (LTV):** This metric measures the amount of loan in reference to the total value of the property that the borrower is willing to buy. This also helps the lender to minimize his lending risk and is calculated in this way:

Imagine Elizabeth wants to purchase a property valued at $500,000 and applies for a loan amount of $350,000. Her LTV ratio will be:

LTV = (loan amount/total property value) * 100

LTV = ($350,000/$500,000) * 100

LTV = 70% (which will most likely help Elizabeth to secure her loan as a general rule of thumb is that the LTV ratio should not be higher than 80%)

b. **Credit Scoring:** You might already be aware of this. Credit scoring is a score that helps analyze the creditworthiness of a borrower and helps the lender make good financial decisions and approval or denial of loan applications. Mostly, lenders use credit scores provided by FICO® and VantageScore®. Usually, the credit score is based on:

- Credit utilization

- Types of credit used

- Length of credit history

- Payment history

- Credit accounts and so on

c. **Credit History:** It's a detailed record of a person's borrowing and repayment history. It helps lenders analyze whether the borrower will be able to pay back the agreed loan amount based on their history. If a person was unable to pay their loans in the past, then their credit history is not good. Keep in mind, that any late payments can result in a poor credit history and the lender might take it seriously.

So, these were all of the crucial aspects of financing real estate transactions. Now, let's take a look at how agencies work and what the crucial aspects of running its affairs, are in relation to the guidelines and regulations imposed by the government. Also, we will discuss the usual business practices involved!

Chapter 5

GENERAL PRINCIPLES OF AGENCY

Agency in real estate means the legal responsibilities that your real estate agent has to fulfill or abide by during any of the real estate transactions. It is very important to understand the essential concepts of this relationship as it helps one to envision the kind of experience, they will have in bringing the buyer and seller together.

We will also add a few examples to illustrate this better. Just like the previous chapters, it's also very important in reference to the exam questions.

Let's first take a look at general agency relationships before we take a look at the technical or legal side.

A. Agency & Non-Agency Relationships

Since we already know that the world of real estate is vivid and there are a lot of aspects that are associated with it, we can see the same thing when it comes to real estate agents. Just like a multitude of ways in which properties exist, real estate agents exist in various forms.

And each form has its own set of responsibilities and obligations. Let's take a detailed look at it:

1. **Types of agents and agencies:** There are multiple types of agents and agencies. These are some of the prominent ones:

TYPES OF AGENTS / AGENCIES

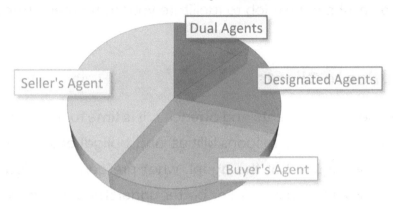

- **Seller's Agent**: an agent representing a seller in any deal.

- **Buyer's Agent**: an agent representing a buyer in any deal.

- **Dual-Agent**: Just like dual agents in the intelligence world, there can exist a situation where the same agent represents both the buyer and the seller and helps them to bring to an agreement.

- **Designated Agents**: As we were discussing just before, an agency can also represent both the buyer and seller. In that case, an agency might designate agents (that it employs) for both buyer and seller. Those are called designated agents.

2. **Other Brokerage Relationships (non-agents):** We have taken a look at what traditional agency setups look like, the one where a buyer or a seller approaches an agency, tells them what they need, and gets their service while paying a commission to the agency. In real estate, there can exist several other brokerage roles where there is no agency involved. Some of them are:

- **Transactional Brokers:** As it sounds, these kinds of brokers are not involved in bringing the buyer and seller together. Instead, they are more concerned with the transaction side of the deal, taking care of essential paperwork, and guiding the client (buyer, seller, or both) financially.

- **Facilitators:** These are people who facilitate but do not take any sides. These are neutral people who have a job to facilitate your agreement, transaction, or even transfer.

B. Agent's Duties to Clients

Having discussed the type of agents and agencies, it is time for us to take a look at what is more important: the agent's responsibilities and obligations. It entails answers to questions like what is required of the agent, what are certain obligations that every agency must comply with, and so on. For better understanding, we have summarized our outline so that you remember all that will be asked of you in the exam very easily.

Also, so that your knowledge about real estate Increases; it's the thing that matters more than this exam. Because if you are dedicated, you will, eventually, pass the exam and start your professional career.

But if you are starting with a mindset that believes that the better we know, the more educated we are about what we are selling (your services as a real estate agent), we can always expect good results. In simple words, knowing more elevates your performance in this career. With that being said, let's take a look at some of the basic duties of agents.

1. **Fiduciary Responsibilities:** Fiduciary means a trustee. As a real estate agent, your goal is not to make money but to provide your clients with the best of your care and loyalty. And that care should be genuine because good always attracts good. If you feel your client is making a wrong choice, then you should tell them why is it so. Because as an agent, your priority is to ensure that your client gets the best results from whatever they seek from you. An easy way to do this is to be kind and promise yourself to always think about the client. Also, it is your duty to maintain the client's privacy by keeping personal information, or any other things that your client doesn't want anyone else to know about, confidential.

2. **Traditional Agency Duties (COALD):** There is a common acronym (abbreviation) in the world of real estate: COALD. Each word in this acronym represents a duty that every agent must follow. Let's see what they are:

- **Care** – All agents must express keen care for their clients in all of their dealings, making wise decisions that will help them eventually, and discussing with them freely.

- **Obedience** – All agents must always be obedient to whatever the client requires of them. It is because the "customer is always right". Follow all of their instructions and don't add things or decisions from your own.

- **Accounting** – Your number one goal is to earn the trust of your clients. To do so, an agent must always provide complete and transparent reports on funds and properties that have been entrusted to them by their clients. All agents must stay accountable at all costs because this is what affects their reputation in the long run.

- **Loyalty** – All agents must remain loyal to their clients, acting in their best interests, and providing them with a comfortable and smooth experience.

- **Disclosure** – All agents must disclose any information or regulations that they think can affect the stature of their client's transactions or properties. Any information regarding the actual value of a property must always be communicated right from the start.

Now, quick imaginative exercise for you:

"Create a scenario where an agent's failure to adhere to one of the COALD duties results in a legal or ethical dilemma. Explain the consequences of the agent's actions and discuss how the situation could have been avoided if they had followed the duty correctly."

Try answering it for yourself. These are some of examples that will help you to inspire imaginative case scenarios:

Loyalty Duty: An agent represents both the buyer and seller in a real estate transaction without disclosing this dual agency. The agent may prioritize their own interests or the interests of one party over the other, leading to a conflict of interest. This could result in accusations of unfair treatment, breach of fiduciary duty, or even legal action by one or both parties involved. To avoid this, the agent should have disclosed the dual agency and ensured fairness to both parties or recommended separate representation.

Disclosure Duty: An agent fails to disclose known material defects in a property to potential buyers. This omission could lead to buyers purchasing the property unaware of its issues, resulting in dissatisfaction, financial loss, and potentially legal action against the agent for negligence or misrepresentation. To avoid this, the agent should have diligently disclosed all known defects and provided accurate information to the buyers.

Care Duty: An agent neglects to conduct proper due diligence on a property, resulting in misinformation provided to the client. For example, the agent fails to verify zoning regulations or property boundaries, leading the client to make decisions based on inaccurate information. This could lead to financial losses, legal disputes, or damage to the agent's reputation for incompetence. To avoid this, the agent should have conducted thorough research and ensured the accuracy of the information provided to the client.

3. **Power of Attorney and other delegation of authority:** Power of attorney is when authority is given to a real estate agent (or any person) by the client to act on specified, legal, or financial matters in his place. A client might be busy so they will leave certain powers in your lap, for example, to make decisions in his place. While doing this, every agent must abide by the duties that we have discussed above.

C. Creation of Agency/Non-agency Agreements

(Disclosure of conflict of interest)

The good thing about the modern professional world is that almost everything is regulated and legalized. It means that everything, all kinds of dealings, and agreements, has to be backed by paperwork. Because that's proof that defends us from legal action, in case any dispute arises. That's common sense.

1. Agency & Agency Agreements

Similarly, real estate agency as well as non-agency, to run their business affairs smoothly, have to abide by certain obligations that have been designed by the government for their benefit. These agreements can be mentioned:

- Agreed duties

- Rights of involved parties

- Obligations

- Responsibilities

- Or any other term that your client or you may want to add to the agreement.

The key thing to understand here is that the more detailed your agreements are, the more trust you will be able to have, and the more professionalism will reflect from you.

Let's take a sneak peek at some of the important elements involved in these agreements/contracts:

a. **Key Elements of Different Types of Listing Contracts:** As it sounds, listing contracts are simple agreements between a real estate agent/agency/non-agency and the owner of the property. Now, in case, a property owner comes to you or your company's office expressing his wish to sell his property. But he wants you to take care of all that has to be there as he is busy somewhere. Now, he can have several reasons. Let's take a look at some of the common elements:

- **Rights to Sell:** A listing contract can include an agent having rights to act in the place of the owner to sell their property. These rights are given by the owners themselves. Note that, in this case, the agents hold exclusive rights, which means they are entitled to a commission, regardless of whose efforts helped find the buyer.

Example: John is 70 years old and he just wants to sell one of his properties because it is not up to his use. He wants you to sell it, so he gives you exclusive rights, which are prepared by his lawyer. And then John is contacted by one of his friends and she wants to buy his property. In this case of the listing contract, even when John found the buyer, you are still entitled to the commissions because you hold exclusive rights that were given to you by John!

- **Exclusive Agency:** Imagine your client comes to you and he/she wants to sell their house. But he wants to pay commission only if you sell the property instead of him/her finding a buyer. That's an exclusive agency, where the client (seller) holds exclusive rights to sell the property on their own, saving them from paying a commission. Note that, you can still charge them your service charges.

Example: Mary signs an exclusive listing contract with XYZ Realtors (an agency) to sell their property (as they are listing, mostly sellers list it, but there is always room for a company providing services where people can set their ideal requirements and list it so that sellers can contact them, a nice business idea). In case, Mary lands upon a buyer on her own, then she doesn't have to pay any commissions to XYZ Realtors. This is ideal for clients looking for an extra hand in selling their property.

- **Open Listing Contract:** Sometimes, your client might be in a rush to buy or sell a property. In that case, they might require an open listing contract where they have a right to approach multiple agents/brokers or agencies to help them find their property. In this case, the client only has to pay commissions to the agent or agency that helped him/her in finding their buyer or seller (in case they are looking to buy a property). That's why it's called an open listing, commissions open for whoever does the job!

Example: Alex is looking to sell his house so he contacts 2 agents and 2 agencies. Whoever among them brings the buyer will be entitled to the commission.

b. **Key Elements of Buyer Brokerage/Tenant Representation Contracts:** As we mentioned before there can be certain instances where a buyer can be interested in having your brokerage or agency services. In that case, a fiduciary relationship is formed. One that requires you to act in the best interests of the buyer and perform your duties with goodwill and compassion for whatever dreams they hold from this new start. Also, these buyers can be tenants, who legally are entitled to rights to act as a buyer (except ownership, of course) until when the contract expires. These are some of the key elements that are required in these kinds of contracts or agreements:

- **Time duration** of the contract (depending on your client's requirements, you can either specify it or go forward with a general one expressed in months only or by the end of that month)

- **Terms and conditions** regarding the compensation in case a certain thing goes wrong or finding the property gets delayed

- **Duties and obligations** of the agent/agency/non-agency (after the property has been found)

- **Responsibilities and conditions** the buyer (client) has to follow in this overall time duration of the contract)

2. **Disclosure When Acting as Principal or Other Conflicts of Interest:** We have already discussed the importance and involvement of disclosures in the "COALD" section. As an agent or agency, sometimes you can have a personal interest in a deal or you might be representing both the buyer and the seller. Now, that is a conflict of interest that can affect your reputation and the trust involved in the deal.

In this case, it is the responsibility of the agent/agency to seek the consent of both buyer and seller while disclosing to them everything that is to be there, personal interests, reservations, or anything that can affect the overall reputation of the agency.

D. Responsibilities of Agents to Customers and Third Parties

These are the same duties and responsibilities that we have discussed at the start of this chapter. Let's take this moment as a revision because these values are so important not only to understand real estate but to pass the exam.

As a real estate agent/agency, you can be required to follow certain procedures or duties in the best interest of your clients. The most important fiduciary duties are:

- **Loyalty:** Throughout, the real estate transaction, it is the duty of the agent (you) to take care of their client's best interests. In doing so, they must stay loyal to bringing them benefits or value from the transaction.

- **Obedience:** As they say, your customer is always right. As an agent, you must stay obedient to your clients at all costs. It means that you have to guide them and act as per their will. Even in any case, if you have advocated some benefits and changes in the course of plans, and if your client doesn't want it, you must obey their will.

- **Confidentiality:** The best your clients can expect from you is a sense of privacy and confidentiality. As an agent, your fiduciary responsibility is to take decisions that will help promote your client's safety, meaning you should not share any critical information with other fellows, and it should stay between the three parties which are buyer, seller, and agent/agency.

- **Care and Goodwill:** When it comes to expressing care and goodwill, you should maintain a personality where these values are mere words. It's because money will not bring you as much satisfaction as the happiness and trust of a client in this world of estates. You can foster these values by understanding and accepting all of the fiduciary responsibilities mentioned before and after this.

- **Accounting and Transparency:** As we have earlier said, it is important to focus on getting the client's trust. You can do it by staying accountable to them, sharing financial reports with them, disclosing where all of their funds were used, and what was the cost. The more transparency you maintain, the better your reputation will be. Doing all so, while avoiding any unethical behavior.

- **Ethical Standards:** When it comes to ethical standards, it means practicing ethical values as a person such as goodwill, care, trust, and transparency. While, at the same time, practicing ethical guidelines by institutions and regulatory bodies.

- **Honesty**: As they say, honesty is the best policy. In the real estate world, it is a gateway to open more opportunities and foster long-term growth. By staying honest with your clients, you are sticking yourself to the best approach which is where all of your decisions influence long-term goals. Most people fail because they find it welcoming to deceive their clients for short-term profits. Without realizing that it is deterring their reputation in the long-run, because sooner or later, they will find out. You are not the only smart person in this world. So, believe it that honesty will take you places, not just in the real estate world, but in every sphere of your life.

- **Fair dealings**: In the end, all deals that an agent makes, should be fair in nature. It means that it should respect the rights and interests of the three (or more) parties involved such as the buyer, seller, and agent. To keep everything professional, you should not compromise on your fiduciary rights and interests as well.

It is very important for you to consider these fiduciary responsibilities because it is the only way for an agent to become successful in the long run. If you are expecting quick results, then you should keep in mind the fact that "what comes in quickly, goes quickly." You need not memorize these responsibilities. Instead, just understand them, and when the question regarding these appears in your exam, try to answer it with the understood concept, by putting yourself in the underlying case scenario. Follow them for all of your clients, irrespective of their needs as it will only help in climbing up the ladder of success.

E. Termination of Agency

There can be various instances when an agency can be terminated and it can be because of several reasons such as:

- **Expiration of the contract:** As all contracts come with a time duration, an agency is terminated when the contract expires. This can be renewed or extended based on the mutual consent of the agency and its clients.

- **Contract being delivered or completed:** A contract ceases to exist when an agency has delivered the agreed services.

- **Termination because of legal dispute and court order:** We have discussed the importance of disclosure and conflict of interests. Sometimes, a legal dispute can involve the law to terminate your contract depending on the violation an agency has done to the law.

- **Property getting destroyed because of any reason:** Because of natural hazards, misfortunate events, technical fault, or fire, a property can get destroyed. In that case, your contract with a client is terminated. Because there is nothing left to sell. That's why it is important to get properties insured.

- **Because both parties have mutually agreed to end the contract:** In certain cases, there might be no progress or a client might want to end the contract because of their reasons. In that case, when an agency and the client come to a mutual consent, the contract/agreement ceases to exist.

- **Death of the client:** In a misfortunate event, the owner of the property can pass away. That is when the contract is terminated because there is no principal left to provide services to. In case, after the hereditary transfer of titles, the next owner still wants to pursue then another contract can be signed. But the previous one would cease to exist, of course!

In the end, it is really important to understand the core principles of agencies and to know about the different case scenarios that can occur. Visualization always helps. Put yourself in different scenarios and based on the knowledge you have so far (or the chapter you have just read), try to imagine what different scenarios where you might be helping clients out. Imagine a client who wants you to have exclusive selling rights. Then imagine yourself having conflicts of interest. Try to think and answer:

- What will be your answer?

- How will you mitigate the situation?

- How would you maintain the trust and reputation?

- Any dialogues for fun and suspense in the imagination?

With that being said, it is time for us to quickly see another side of disclosures, one that is different from what we have seen so far.

Exercise Questions

1. Mr. Michael hired Agent Smith to sell his property. They agreed on a commission rate of 5%. If the property sells for $300,000, how much commission will Agent Smith earn?

   Use the formula:

Commission = Property Sale Price × Commission Rate

2. Sarah is interested in buying a house and approaches a real estate agent, Maria, to help her find a suitable property. What type of agency relationship exists between Sarah and Maria?

   (A) Principal-Agent   (B) Agent-Subagent

   (C) Dual Agency   (D) Transactional Agency

3. Tom signed a listing agreement with Agent Smith to sell his property. However, before the agreement's expiration date, Tom decided to terminate the contract. What type of termination is this?

   (A) Expiration   (B) Completion

   (C) Termination by force of law   (D) Mutual agreement

Chapter 6

PROPERTY DISCLOSURES

Disclosures and legal requirements related to it are there to help agencies and people involved in these to have a level of trust and transparency throughout the duration of the contract. As it sounds, property disclosures mean that any information related to properties, any defects, or traits that might affect the overall stature of the contract, be disclosed to buyers or sellers so that transparency is maintained.

Understanding property disclosures is a very important aspect of any professional because we have been lamenting the fact ever since we started that it's the goodwill and hard work that pays the best results.

Normally, agents and agencies request a property disclosure from the buyer or seller before the start of the contract. This information can be taken in any way but the most popular one involves handing out forms or questions where multiple options or checkboxes are listed.

If a person is selling their property, it is not necessary that they get a property inspection for their disclosure statement, a property disclosure document.

But if a person is looking to buy a property, they should consider paying some extras for inspection because it is for their best.

A property disclosure statement/form can include information like:

- *Are there any defects that the owner knows of about the property?*

- *Any illegal construction on the property that the owner is aware of?*

- *Whether the house is renovated or any material of minor quality was used in the construction?*

- *Are there any issues like leakages, termites, mold, lead-based paint, or HVAC (Heating, Venting, and Air Conditioning) defects?*

- *Are there any due payments or liens against the property?*

- *Is it situated in a crime or flood zone, or has any murder ever taken place on the property (applicable to limited states)?*

A. Property Condition

In order to get the most out of delivering a successful contract or deal, and to maintain the faith and trust of all the involved parties, professionals must understand the different aspects of property conditions.

1. **A property might fall under a certain category that might warrant any inspections or surveys**. This can be because of many reasons, mainly relating to those factors that can affect the property value such as:

   - Issues relating to structure, construction guidelines, or foundation

   - Issues related to HVAC or water damages

   - Pest infestations

2. **Proposed Uses or Changes:** Also, in any case, that the owner has made amendments to the usage of the property or made any legal violation, then while assessing the property disclosure statement and after the home inspection, real estate professionals open for themselves a gateway of safety and transparency. Also, you should have the eye of a hawk when it comes to inspection of properties on your own. With experience, you will see that you are getting good at it.

Example: Imagine you are having your coffee when a client approaches you, expressing their concern about purchasing a property in an area suitable for mix-usage developments (residential and commercial). But both of you didn't pay enough attention to zoning plans. After the deal was secured, it was discovered that a large complex was to be built nearby which would affect the value of the property where residential construction had already started.

That's a big red flag in a deal!

One more example. You are approached by a client who wants to buy a property with a swimming pool. But the area they are looking into has legal barriers so it would be nice and welcoming of you to inform them about these kinds of property usages that can trigger inquiries about public and private land use controls.

B. Environmental Issues Requiring Disclosures

Since we live in a world full of climate change happenings, more and more policies are being laid down to help mitigate CO_2 emissions. The same is happening to the real estate sector as in every other industry.

Therefore, when it comes to property disclosures, it is very important to keep environmental considerations in mind and follow the guidelines of different authorities.

Also, these environmental disclosures directly relate to the property value and desirability. For example, one person would not want to buy a property where contamination has occurred or one that is situated around a landfill of toxic chemicals or industrial waste. Also, there can be asbestos or lead-based paints used on the property which are in strict violation of the EPA standards.

A similar case occurred in 2016 when a real estate agent failed to disclose the contamination of land to the buyer. Later, the buyer discovered it and sued the agent which resulted in him paying heavy fines and losing reputation in the real estate market.

C. Government Disclosure Requirements (LEAD)

Similar to environmental considerations, certain regulations are imposed by the government to help regulate and run the affairs of the people smoothly. LEAD

CHAPTER 6 | PROPERTY DISCLOSURES

requirements related to all regulations related to disclosing lead-based paint usage on the property, especially those that were constructed before 1978.

These regulations are mostly monitored by the EPA (Environmental Protection Agency) to help promote user safety and sustainability. Under their regulations, an agent can be required to collect necessary forms and data pertaining to the disclosure of information on any lead-based paint usage. Even in case, one of your clients happens to have purchased a property with lead usage, it is the duty of the agent to guide them to mitigate the situation by minimizing the health and safety risks (implementing effective control strategies).

Many lawsuits have been filed against agents who failed to disclose the usage of lead-based paints to home buyers. Sooner or later, they are going to discover it so it's better to follow the regulations and notify them. So, you are safe from heavy fines, penalties, and a loss of hard-earned reputation.

D. Material Facts and Defects Disclosures

We have already discussed the importance of disclosing the defects and material facts (especially those that were used in the construction) to the buyers or sellers so that there is no dispute in the near future.

These two factors directly relate to the property value. For example, a person might not want to pay the asked price because they think the material used is of minor quality and they would want to upgrade it.

Also, a person might not want to buy a property with defects that they came to know about before closing the contract, even if it was at the last second. Keep in mind that they have a right to back out of any deal, even at the last moment, if they think certain information was not disclosed to them.

For revision, material facts can include:

- Structural issues

- Water damages

PSI NATIONAL REAL ESTATE LICENSE EXAM PREP

- Zoning restrictions

- Pest Infestations

- Lawsuits or pending payments against the property, and so on.

In the end, it is your duty as a real estate professional to disclose any information that can affect the value or fairness of the deal, and that can eventually save you from making any violations against the law, and thus protecting your reputation. It is important to follow ethical standards at all costs.

Because it is your utmost job to deliver the best and the most comfortable experience to your clients, and failing to do so can result in a bad career. Thus, better to know first, than to learn by repeating the same mistake. Now, we have taken a look at different forms of contracts here and there in this guide as paperwork (contracts/agreements) is everywhere. So how about a detailed discussion on it?

Chapter 7

CONTRACTS

We have mentioned a lot about contracts here and there in this book. This topic not only forms most of what you can expect in the exam (a good strategy is to be overall prepared regardless of where the exam comes from) but also the knowledge you will need the most in your day-to-day life as a professional realtor.

Its simple definition would be legal agreements that bind the seller and buyer together. Since there is the word "legal" in it, it is enforceable by law, meaning that in case of a lawsuit, if one party violates the terms of the contract, they can be subjected to a penalty.

As we have overly stated, it can affect one's reputation as an agent too.

Contracts will be everywhere so we felt that it would be a nice idea to make a separate chapter on it. We will try to cover topics that we haven't delved deeply into before. So, let's try to explore contracts from the legal side first.

A. General Knowledge of Contract Law

We know what a contract is. But as we were discussing in the introduction, there is a dire need to understand the legal aspects of contracts.

Let's start by seeing what the general requirements are:

1. **Requirements for Validity:** There can be different requirements that must be fulfilled for a contract to stand legitimate depending on the case scenario. But there are some requirements that you will mostly see in all of the contracts.

And as a professional real estate agent, it is your utmost duty to verify that everything is as per the regulations, and in the best interest of all the involved parties.

These common requirements are:

- There should be a general agreement between the buyer and the seller. A general agreement means that a contract should have a clear property price given by one party, while the other one should agree 100% with it.

- A certain consideration should be paid by both parties for trust to be maintained. It can be a simple advance payment from the buyer to the seller which has to be returned in case the contract gets violated.

- All contracts must stay in line with the legal regulations and practices, and must not involve anything that serves an illegal purpose. If you are an agent and you know something that can get one of the parties behind bars, it is your duty to inform both of the parties so a certain conflict can be avoided in the near future.

- In the end, both parties should be above the legal age and maturity level to enter a contract.

Now, there are certain factors that go along with these requirements for contracts. We need to take a look at them as well.

2. **Factors affecting enforceability of contracts:** In order to protect the rights of both parties, there are certain regulations and frameworks that must be followed in order for a contract to be legitimate. In some cases, the rights of a party can be violated by the other party, or any other prohibited means can be used to force someone for their motives. Among these factors, the general ones that affect the enforceability of a contract are:

- **Fraud or Misinformation:** A contract is terminated in case one party commits any fraud or conceals vital information regarding the property from both the agent and the other party (person).

- A contract can stand as illegitimate in case one party **threatens or pressurizes** the other party. But this is rare and one should have good evidence to press charges against the violator.

- In rare cases, one can use their position to influence the terms and conditions of a contract in their favor. If certain evidence is there, then in that case, the contract ceases to exist as well.

3. **Void, Voidable, and Unenforceable Contracts:** A contract can exist in many types depending on the underlying case scenario. Since we are exploring the legal side of contracts for now, these are the three types in which a contract can often exist (especially when we are considering rights and their violations as we were discussing just before this):

- **Void Contracts:** Any contract that stands as void right from the beginning. For example, it can miss certain general requirements. So, it will be a void contract right from the start.

- **Voidable Contracts:** Any contract that was legal when it was signed but later stands as void because a certain fraud was discovered or threats were made to any party. The most common of these is when a property gets listed and everything is okay until verifications of documents are made and one discovers that there is a serious dispute in the ownership of the property. Now, that's a fraud so the contract will stand as voidable.

- **Unenforceable Contract:** We have already discussed the factors affecting the enforceability in courts such as a contract can miss so much of the legal requirements that even a case is not possible on it. Therefore, it's a contract that cannot be enforced.

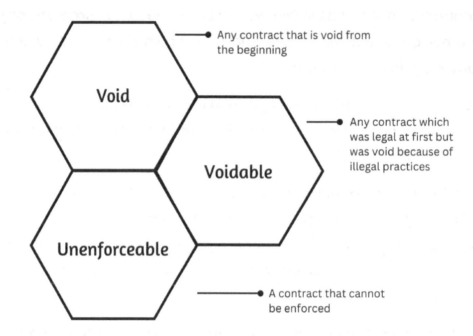

4. **Rights and Obligations of a Party to a Contract:** It is important to take some time to consider the terms and conditions for entering a contract. Once your client or you (in case you have exclusive rights from them) have considered all the points of the contract and they have been accepted by the other party, the contract now requires two things from both of the parties. It means that both buyer and seller (even agent/agency in case they were mentioned to perform any duty) are subject to follow and understanding:

- **Rights:** Both parties hold rights that are entitled and agreed upon by both of them and are mentioned in the terms of the contract.

- **Obligations:** Both parties are obliged to fulfill whatever is required from them, relating to both the contract and law.

These can generally include elements like:

- Goodwill and demonstration of faith in the other party

- Sticking with the regulatory framework to ensure the legality of the process

- To demonstrate confidentiality for the better interest of each other

- All the terms of the contract

Let's now take a look at two more types of contracts. As we mentioned earlier, there can be numerous types of contracts, and the easy way to remember them is to categorize them by case scenarios. For example, when we were discussing factors affecting the enforceability of the contract, we discussed when contracts go void.

Now that we have reached the point in this 'contract law' story where a contract has been signed, let's see its types in relation to execution (case scenario here).

5. **Executory & Executed Contracts:** These two terms appear similar to each other but they are very different in meaning.

   Executory contracts are ones where one party still has to fulfill certain obligations. Therefore, the contract cannot be marked complete as certain actions are still to be taken by one of the parties.

   For example, an executory contract occurs when a property is listed by the seller and a buyer makes him/her an offer. The moment the seller accepts the offer, the executory contract starts, until the moment when the buyer has completed all of his obligations.

   When all of the obligations are completed, that's what we call an **executed contract.** It can include general elements like:

   - A meeting where a transfer is made to the buyer after all legal documents have been signed

   - Recording of the transfer deed by the municipal office which makes the transfer legitimate

   - Seller submits the possession to the buyer leaving real property and personal property such as furniture or paintings if it was agreed to in the terms

   - The buyer makes the complete payment to the seller

6. **Notice, Delivery, & Acceptance of Contracts:** In order to ensure a smooth running process in real estate contracts, there are certain steps to follow at certain stages of the contract.

These are:

- **Notice** of contracts helps notify all the involved parties about the terms and conditions of the contract. It also notifies them when the contract started to exist. The general aim of notices is to ensure that everyone involved is aware of their responsibilities and rights.

    For example, a seller can request additional time to amend the desired repairs that the buyer highlighted and that they agreed to in the contract. Now, he has to send a notice to the buyer and seek their consent for a time extension.

- **Delivery** of contracts is when the contract is delivered (copies are distributed) to all of the concerned parties to inform everyone about the contract and its terms. The basic intention is to bring them to an agreement and foster goodwill that all of them will be bound by what they agreed to, a gentle reminder.

- As it sounds, **acceptance** of a contract occurs when it has been signed after evaluation of terms and conditions by both parties.

7. **Breach of Contract & Remedies for Breach:** Let's not take a look at when a contract gets breached and some examples to help you understand how to remediate breaches in real estate. You should note here that these breaches can be of various types, ranging from legal ones to those relating to duress:

- Improper disclosure of material defects by the seller can result in the buyer losing interest in the property. Also, it's a breach of their rights.

    To remediate it, the buyer can request an initial deposit and in case they have suffered any financial or mental losses, they can also file a lawsuit against the seller.

- Oftentimes, the buyer or seller can fail to submit the payment or any other obligations by the agreed timeline.

  To remediate it, the non-breaching party can request their financial deposits (if any) or offer an extension in case the buyer presents them with a valid reason and compensation.

8. **Termination, Rescission, & Cancellation of Contracts:** We have already discussed a few of the case scenarios relating to the termination of contracts. As it sounds, it is when a contract is terminated or ceases to exist. This ending of a contract is adjoined with the mutual consent of both parties, who because of whatever reason they had want to end the contract before a full execution of a contract can occur.

  Rescission occurs when a contract is canceled or terminated as if it never existed. It can occur because of reasons like fraud, fundamental mistakes, any threat or pressure to the seller, and so on. For example, Vince is looking to buy a large piece of agricultural land. He agrees on the price but until the last moment, his inquiries led him to know that the soil quality is poor for farming. So, he seeks the rescission from the contract. And this the contract becomes void as if it never existed.

  Cancellation is similar to the both above terms, except for the fact that it can exist in a unilateral form as well. For example, a seller might cancel a contract in case the buyer fails to oblige by the agreed terms, or if they are unable to arrange the financing for the purchase.

  Also, in case a seller's time and resources are wasted during the duration of the contract, they can file a lawsuit which is most likely to be compensated by the court. If a situation like this occurs, it is good to seek a real estate lawyer for better and more detailed guidance about the law.

  One must not hesitate to do this as an agent/agency/non-agency since networking is another key to success in this real estate world.

9. **Electronic Signatures & Paperless Transactions:** Up till now, we have taken a good look at the general elements of contracts, their types, laws associated with them, and

good practices that you can follow to endure your journey after you have passed your exam.

It is time for us to take a brief look at what happens once the contracts have been signed, passed the termination/cancellation phase, turned into a transaction, or actually, favored it.

There are two important things (that you might already be aware of) to add to our preparation here:

- **Electronic Signatures**, as it sounds, is the signature of a person in electronic or digital form. Something that can be signed from a device instead of the typical signature on paper. These can be legally acceptable If they provide the beholder's consent and approval of the signature.

- **Paperless transactions** relate to transactions that are electronic or digital in nature, and that don't incorporate transactions being recorded on paper. Instead, all of the information is stored on servers and can be accessed from anywhere in the world.

  Both of these practices are getting more and more common as technology progresses and people at a global scale embrace the power of digital finance. Also, with De-Fi on its way, who knows we might be having real estate payments in digital tokens if one day we can regulate them.

10. Bilateral vs Unilateral Contracts (option agreements):

Bilateral Contracts mean a contract that involves both parties performing certain duties and making promises to each other. A contract in which both buyer and seller are involved. Its most common example is a purchase agreement. It's an agreement where one party promises to sell the property (seller) and the other one expresses its will to buy it (buyer).

Unilateral vs Bilateral Contracts

Bilateral	**Unilateral**
● Involves both parties	● Involves one party
● A common example is a purchase agreement	● Options agreement
● Promisor & Promisee	● Offeror and Offeree

Unilateral Contract, on the other hand, represents a promise that is made by one party instead of both the party. In unilateral contracts, there are two types of people:

- Offeror (making the offer)

- Offeree (performing the offer)

Its most common example is an options agreement. It's similar to options trading or contracts that are used in almost all kinds of markets, from commodities to assets. In real estate, an options agreement works when a seller (offeror) offers an offeree (buyer) a proposition that he/she has the option to buy their property within a specific time duration if they pay a certain option fee. Now, this favors the buyer as they are unilaterally agreeing to perform the offer but it is not a must. They have an option to end the contract by just losing their option fee.

B. Contract Clauses, Including Amendments & Assets

Apart from contracts, there can be some additional documents or clauses that go along with the main contract. It is usually to cover any missing information that was initially not distributed in the contract. These are contract clauses. And they can exist in many forms, depending on the underlying case scenario.

Below are some of the most common ones that you can expect to see everywhere in your professional career:

- **Contingency Clause:** A clause containing terms and conditions that must be met at all costs in order for the contract to stand legit. In case, the requirements are not provided by the party, the contract gets terminated without penalty to each party.

Its most common case scenario is when the contract has been signed that a buyer will buy a property using a mortgage loan. But when weeks pass by and the seller gets concerned, they issue a contingency clause mentioning a certain deadline for the buyer to secure their loan. Failure to do so will result in the termination of the contract.

It has several types such as:

1. **Inspection Contingency Clause** – sometimes a buyer can request an inspection of the property by a professional inspector. That's when they need to send an inspection contingency clause to the seller.

2. **Financing Contingency Clause** – it is simply a clause in which a buyer can back out of a deal in case they are unable to arrange the funds for the property.

3. **Appraisal Contingency Clause** – this protects the buyer again as they can back out of a contract in case the price does not go beyond the agreed value. Also, a buyer can renegotiate the purchase price here in case the seller's claims are not correct.

4. **Title Contingency Clause** – this is submitted when the buyer wants a clear title before transferring the whole funds or before the closing date of the contract.

5. **Earnest Money Deposit Clause** – it simply refers to when a buyer has to deposit earnest money to gain the faith and trust of the seller. They can deposit in an escrow account where they are legally entitled to their deposit in case no violations to back out of the obligations are made from their end.

There are two more kinds of additional documents that also (similar to clauses) go along with the main contract/agreement.

1. **Amendments:** As it sounds, there are any additional amendments to the main contract that are to be signed by both parties in order to stand legitimate.

2. **Addenda:** In case any problem was not highlighted in the main contract or any contingency not being submitted or filed, the buyer or seller can opt for any additional requirements.

Its most common example is a 'seller disclosure addendum' which simply requests the seller to disclose any issues or damages to the property as we previously discussed in detail, pest infestations, water damages, etc.

C. Offer/Purchase Agreements

Offer and purchase agreements are everywhere in this world of real estate. From expressing general interest to making an offer to the seller, you need to understand the underlying important concepts that we have summarized for you.

A simple way to define an offer is when the buyer sends an offer which can include conditions for acceptance.

And purchase agreement is an agreement between the buyer and the seller.

Let's start by seeing the general requirements.

1. **General Requirements:** There are some general requirements that have to be fulfilled for an agreement to stand out. These are:

   - The offeror (a person making the offer) and the offeree (a person receiving the offer) must be on the same page, and agree on clear terms, and price, in order to enter a legal contract or agreement.

   - There should be some considerations made to foster faith and trust in the agreement. Considerations can be things, money, or services promised to one party by the other so that they stick with their promise of going forward with the deal.

- Once again, both parties should be of legal age and maturity in order for a purchase agreement to commence.

2. **When Offer Becomes Binding:** Whenever you see the word or question of "when", you should know that there is an impeccable aspect of timing involved. Just like that, it is crucial for a real estate agent to understand when an offer becomes binding. The process goes like this:

- An offer by the offeror has been communicated with the buyer with a specific time deadline for them to accept.

- When the buyer issues a **receipt of acceptance** stating that he agrees with the offeror's terms and price.

- That is when an offer becomes binding.

  For example, Michael offers to purchase Sarah's house by 5:00 PM Thursday. He communicates his offer to her. Sarah accepts Michael's offer and contacts her via landline to notify him about her acceptance (receipt of acceptance being issued). An offer becomes binding!

3. **Contingencies:** Please refer to section "B" of this chapter for a detailed discussion on contingencies. For revision, these are simply conditions that have to be fulfilled so that a contract is not terminated.

4. **Time is of the Essence:** It is a very famous saying that is common and used all around the world. It implies the underlying discipline that has to be followed in all kinds of agreements, and deadlines that are to be met under all circumstances. If one fails to do that, chances are that their contract or agreement might get terminated. A common example is when people showcase a loan to finance their purchase but end up failing to get that loan. Thus, a contract gets terminated, owing to the wastage of time of the involved parties.

In the end, these were some crucial aspects of offers that you should keep in mind. Now, let's see some more types of offers and some more underlying case scenarios.

D. Counteroffers/Multiple Offers

Now every time you can expect your journey to be smooth. Sometimes there can be suspense and drama in your dealings with clients, where everything doesn't go like a buyer contact and makes an offer, and the seller agrees to it. Not every time it is going to happen. For example:

- **Counteroffers** occur when a buyer makes an offer to a seller and it gets rejected because the seller wants different terms. For example, Emily sends an offer of $400,000 for a house but the owner rejects it and sends her a counteroffer of $450,000 that she can accept, reject, or counter within a specific time duration.

- **Multiple offers** can also occur from time to time with a seller receiving multiple offers for the same property. That's when they need to apply their knowledge or they can ask you out for your services. It is your duty to detail them on the prospects of different deals and help them find the offer that works for their best interests.

So, these were all the sides and faces of contracts. In case, some concepts were difficult for you to grab at once, you can reread them freely. The more you know, the better you will be able to pitch.

Now, let's take a quick tour of leasing and managing properties because a lot of clients come from this sector. As there are more tenants than buyers!

Some Fun Questions to See How Prepared You Are!

1. Define a "voidable contract" and give an example.

2. Describe three common contingencies in a real estate purchase agreement with their importance.

3. What is the difference between a counteroffer and a multiple offer situation in real estate transactions? How do they impact buyers and sellers?

4. What is a bilateral contract? Give a real estate example.

Chapter 8

LEASING & PROPERTY MANAGEMENT

In this chapter, we are going to discuss another, seemingly running side of the real estate world because there are always some requirements for leasing and managing properties, no matter which state you are from.

Leasing relates to the submission of property for a lease or renting it out in the expectation of a certain return that mostly occurs in monthly payments by the tenants.

This inflow of customers to a property creates room for certain repairs to be made, or sometimes, one might have to even adjust the space.

Let's not confuse things up and jump straight into discussing some important elements of leasing and how best to manage a property.

This knowledge is essential not just for future agents or agencies, but for everyone who has something to do with properties, can be a buyer, seller, or even some research professor.

A. Basic Concepts/Duties of Property Management

In simple words, property management requires a person to take care of it, maintain it, look for any damages, and find necessary repairs, with a purpose to help protect its value, and utilization, and to make it compliant with laws and obligations as we have discussed in the previous chapters.

Some basic duties one can expect are:

- *To ensure that the property is maintained properly and the overall condition is protected or good.*

- *To maintain relations with tenants and address both parties' concerns (tenant/owner) or questions promptly.*

- *To collect rent payments as agreed in the lease agreement.*

- *To take care of paperwork related to the lease process such as preparing lease agreements, renewal of terms, and even when an agreement gets terminated.*

B. Lease Agreements

As we were discussing you might be required to perform a duty where you will be assembling and distributing a lot of documents (in your professional career) that we can summarize as lease agreements, renewal of terms as when the rent increases, warnings, and so on.

But before that, you need to know these 4 types in which a lease can exist:

- **Percentage lease** *means that the owner will take a certain percentage from the tenant's sales or business. This can occur in the case of shops and commercial properties mostly.*

- **Gross lease** *is a type of lease in which the tenant is responsible for paying the rent while the owner takes care of insurance, taxes, and repairs.*

- **Net lease** *occurs when the tenant is responsible for paying the rent as well as taking care of insurance, taxes, and repairs.*

- **Ground lease** *can occur in certain cases. It is simply a lease agreement where an owner rents the land for construction for a good set of years.*

Mostly, you will see lease agreements based on these types. For good practice, you can imagine yourself dealing with a client who seeks to sign a percentage lease with someone. Or any situation and try to imagine you will act out in the situation, what will be your go-to words to convince, your body language, and so on.

Back to square one, we now know what a lease agreement is and its types. Let's now see what are the elements that you can add in your lease agreements:

- **Rent amount or payment terms** are the must of every lease agreement. The rent payment should be clear with a deadline for payment along with any extra requirements from the buyer (if any).

- **The duration of the lease and renewal terms** should also be added to the lease agreement. The renewal terms are mostly there to suggest a rent increase, particularly after every year.

- **Maintenance and repairs guidelines** should be clearly stated as to who is responsible for the insurance, taxes, and general maintenance of the property. Mostly the owners take this charge but in the case of a net lease, the tenants can also be held liable for the maintenance and repairs.

- **Restrictions** on property usage can also be included in case the owner wants certain standards and behavior to be followed around in a neighborhood. Also, terms and conditions referring to the inspection of property by the owner, the usual time after it can occur, can be added to the lease agreement.

- **Security Deposits & actions** in case of late fees can also be added to the lease agreement. Any deposit that is provided for security of the deal is a security deposit which will be returned to the tenant once the agreement gets terminated. Note that, in case the tenant is responsible for any damages, the damage costs can be deducted from the security deposit, mostly when they are leaving and the owner inspects the property.

These were some of the key elements that can be included in the lease agreement. It depends on the general requirements of your clients. In case of any legal disputes, it will be wiser to consult a real estate lawyer.

Let's now see the rights and obligations involved in property leasing.

C. Landlord & Tenant Rights & Obligations

There are certain rights that can be exercised by both the parties, tenants and owners, during the duration of the lease agreement or contract. These rights and obligations are backed by the law and any violations can occur in a lawsuit resulting in penalties and punishment.

To become a successful property manager, there are a few values that you need to remember, and that must be enforced in all of the property contracts.

Let's start from the rights:

✓ *Landlords have a right to inspect the property, collect their rent payments, and enforce terms and obligations as agreed by the tenant in the lease agreement.*

✓ *Tenants have a right to spend their lives quietly and peacefully and the standards of the property are up to the mark. Also, they have a right to get timely repairs of damages in case the landlord is liable to those in the lease agreement.*

These were the rights that had to be ensured. There are also some obligations involved in the process:

✓ *Landlords are obliged to take care of all the tenant's rights, from providing habitable conditions to a maintained property.*

✓ *Tenants are obliged to follow the terms, guidelines, and deadlines to make sure that the lease agreement flows smoothly.*

The key thing to exercise here is the lease agreement and make sure that it gets followed at all costs, doing so while staying compliant with the rules and regulations. Let's take a brief look at what your responsibilities can be, as a property manager.

D. Property Manager Fiduciary Responsibilities

Just like the previous fiduciary (trustee) responsibilities that we discussed, as a property manager, you are required to maintain certain standards, encapsulated within a number of responsibilities that you can have, all that together help enforce the lease agreement in its best capacity.

Sometimes, we use a bit of legal language to define or explain anything or ideas here. It is done because of a purpose so you get used to it.

Now, some of the responsibilities that you can expect as a property manager are:

- ✓ *Your number one job is to stay loyal to your client (tenant/landlord/or both) and act in their best interests. Even in case you have a conflict of interest, you have to ignore it to promote a healthy lease agreement.*

- ✓ *You have to act in a careful manner, expressing your diligence throughout the negotiations and signing of the lease contract.*

- ✓ *In the end, you have to stay accountable, especially to the property owner, sharing an income record with them, and making sure they suffer no financial losses.*

Let's take a look at one last element that goes general instead of being personal.

E. ADA & Fair Housing Compliance

It is the right of the people to enjoy equal rights. The same goes for the housing compliances. As a property owner, one should not discriminate against tenants based on their profiles. Instead, they are required to facilitate all kinds of tenants, especially those who are disabled.

For that specific purpose, the Americans with Disabilities Act (ADA) is there to protect the rights of accessible living and from any discrimination against disabled people.

Some of the ADA and Fair Housing compliances can require:

- *A property should be accessible to disabled people including the designs and standards*

- *Accessible entrances and parking*

- *A property should have some space left for a common area*

Also, there should be no discrimination based on:

- *Race*

- *Color or sex*

- *Religion*

- *Nationality*

- *Family Status*

- *And disabilities*

Understanding the FHA & ADA

NO DISCRIMINATION
BASED ON

—**1**—	—**2**—
Color or race	Nationality
—**3**—	—**4**—
Marital Status	Any disability

All of these regulations are there to ensure that the rights of the people get delivered to the people. Failing to comply with these regulations can result in legal action along with heavy penalties.

With that being said, you now know the general features and all the aspects that can be expected in the journey of a professional property manager. Let's now move on to discussing the transfer of titles and related principles in detail.

Exercise Questions

1. *Define a gross lease and provide an example.*

2. *Calculate the total monthly rent for a property under a net lease if the base rent is $1,500 per month, and the tenant is responsible for $200 per month in property taxes and $100 per month in insurance.*

    Use the formula:

    Total Rent = Base Rent + Property Taxes + Insurance

3. *Provide an example of how a property manager can breach their fiduciary duties.*

Chapter 9

TRANSFER OF TITLES

We keep repeating things that you will see the most when you start your career as a professional agent. Transfer of titles is one of them. Everywhere deals are being made and contracts signed, and most of them when a purchase occurs, are relatable to the transfer of ownership from one person to the other.

We have outlined all the important things that will help you to fully understand the topic of transfers and the ownership saga!

Let's start with the introductory elements!

A. Title Insurance

We have seen that titles hold immense importance. However, wherever there exist wonders, there is some malware and some treachery as well. To counter that, real estate bolsters policies that help protect the buyer from a significant loss.

1. ***What is insured against:*** *The simplest among those is getting title insurance which can occur after a transfer has been made, some forgery can be spotted, and so on.*

   The three most common reasons for disputes that we have seen all around the world are:

   - ***Forged Documents***, *there are a multitude of cases regarding this in the whole market.*

   - ***Undisclosed Heirs***, *you can see a lot of them as well in the courts and news and so on.*

- **Errors in Public Records,** sometimes there can be serious mistakes or loss of track in the public records. Though these cases are rare.

To make the information that is coming ahead exciting, we have a little exercise that you can do. Trust us, this does matter as we welcome you back to our imaginative play:

"Imagine you face a scenario where the property owner discovers the bad news that the previous owner of the same property had forged signatures on the contract/deed. From those three types, which one does it represent, and how you will explain to every owner that they should get title insurance!"

2. **Title Searches/Abstracts & Chain of Titles:** It simply refers to the process that is followed by the insurance companies where they go in this sequence.

   - A thorough search of the title records with the purpose of identifying any malpractice or forgery or any other issues with the title of the property.

   - Title abstracts examination takes place in the same thorough fashion. These are any supporting evidence to the title (ownership) such as liens, conveyances, or any other supporting material.

   - In the end, to confirm the validity of the title, the insurance companies run a deep research on the chain of titles which indicates the chain of owners from current to one before him, and so on.

3. **Marketable vs Insurable Titles:** basically, there are two kinds of titles. The first one is a marketable title, one free from any legal disputes or claims, one that is ready to transfer to the next owner.

   The other one is the insurable title. It is also marketable but buyers might have a slight hesitation in buying, but apart from that, sellers have protection from huge losses. So, it's a win-win situation for them.

4. **Potential Title Problems & Resolutions:** As they say, no matter how much we try to achieve perfection, there is always room for human error. Similarly, in real estate, no

matter how thorough one's investigation is as an insurance company or an agent, agency, or just personal investigation, there is always room for some errors to exist. It can happen rarely but as a professional, it's not a good idea to skip this topic.

Most of the problems are commonly caused by these reasons:

- *Boundary disputes as you might have guessed*

- *Unresolved liens*

- *Undisclosed information that can make the title status disputed.*

And that's it.

We have a short exercise for you so it is easier for you to solve assumption-based questions in your exams.

"Analyze a case study of a property with a boundary dispute. Try to google it or ask anyone from the industry. Now imagine yourself in this situation and try to think why did the dispute occur in the first place and what would have been done to have avoided it."

A sample example of a complete case study is given below:

Case scenario

The Smiths, a married couple, recently purchased a beautiful suburban home in a quiet neighborhood. However, their excitement quickly turned into frustration when they discovered discrepancies in the property's boundaries, leading to disputes with their neighbors, the Johnsons. Let's see what happened and how the issue was resolved.

Background

The Smiths conducted a survey of their property shortly after moving in, only to find that the fence separating their backyard from the Johnsons' property encroached several feet onto their land. The Johnsons, unaware of this discrepancy, initially disputed the survey results, claiming historical ownership of the disputed area.

Challenges

1. **Lack of accurate boundary documentation:** Neither party possessed clear and definitive documentation outlining the precise boundaries of their respective properties.

2. **Emotional tensions:** The discovery of the boundary dispute strained the relationship between the Smiths and the Johnsons, making it challenging to resolve the issue.

3. **Legal complexities:** Resolving boundary disputes often involves navigating intricate legal frameworks, including property laws, easements, and possession.

Steps Taken

1. **Consultation with Real Estate Attorney:** The Smiths sought advice from a reputable real estate attorney specializing in boundary disputes. The attorney reviewed relevant documents, including the property deed, surveys, and local zoning ordinances, to assess the situation.

   The attorney explained the legal rights and responsibilities of both parties and outlined potential avenues for resolution.

2. **Mediation:** Recognizing the importance of preserving neighborly relations, the Smiths and the Johnsons agreed to participate in mediation facilitated by a neutral third-party mediator.

   During mediation sessions, both parties had the opportunity to voice their concerns, express their desired outcomes, and explore potential compromises. The mediator facilitated constructive dialogue, encouraged empathy and understanding, and helped the parties reach a mutually acceptable resolution.

3. **Boundary Adjustment:** After thorough discussions and negotiations, the Smiths and the Johnsons agreed to a boundary adjustment that reflected the true property lines as determined by a licensed surveyor. The parties signed a legally binding

agreement outlining the revised boundaries and any necessary modifications to existing structures, such as fences or landscaping.

4. **Documentation and Compliance:** The revised boundaries were officially documented and recorded with the appropriate governmental authorities to ensure legal validity. Both parties committed to complying with the terms of the boundary adjustment agreement, including maintaining the newly established boundaries and refraining from future encroachments.

Outcome

Through proactive communication, legal guidance, and collaborative problem-solving, the Smiths and the Johnsons successfully resolved their boundary dispute in a manner that satisfied both parties. By prioritizing mutual respect and cooperation, they not only clarified property boundaries but also preserved neighborly harmony for years to come.

B. Deeds

We have discussed them before. Deeds are simply legal documents indicating a transfer of property from a grantor (owner) to a grantee (buyer) and are crucial for all kinds of transfers, relating to those of real property, of course.

They can be in any format, written or typed, though the former is used more as it adds to the trust factor. Let's take a look at the general features of deeds:

1. *Purpose of Deed: The purpose of this legal document is to pass the ownership status of real property from one person to another. They can be buyers, investors, or even heirs, depending on the underlying case scenario. In this simple process, two things should be ensured by all kinds of parties involved (agents/professionals):*

   - *There should be a mutual acceptance by the grantor and grantee. As we discussed in the previous chapter, there should be no involvement of forgery, threat, or forcing someone because if the grantor has title insurance, chances are that they will be protected. For you, it can seriously affect your reputation.*

- *Since it is legal, it should be written in a legal language. A wise advice here is to consult a real estate lawyer or any professional while writing a deed and signing it.*

2. **Types of deeds and when used:** *There are certain types and case scenarios in which deeds are used. These types are for the protection of the grantor (owner) of the property (in this whole book, property refers to real property). Let's take a look at a few of the most common types and the level of protection they grant to the grantor.*

   - **General Warranty Deeds:** *This is a sort of legal document in which the grantor makes certain promises to the grantee, such as in case of dispute, the grantor will protect the grantee (buyers/investors/heirs) against any legal claim of the land. The grantor certifies that there is no issue with it and that even if it existed, they will defend it and help the grantee in case any claims are made. They do so by issuing* **covenants** *(legal promises) and* **warranties** *to the grantee. General warranty deeds provide the best protection to the grantee.*

   - **Special Warranty Deeds:** *Imagine the same case scenario for a general warranty deed. But this time, the grantor does not provide help in case of legal claim and certifies that there is no issue or defect with the property in his/her lifetime only.*

     That's why it's a special warranty, one that is limited to the grantor's lifetime only. It offers less protection than general warranty deeds, and one should investigate the chain of titles of the property or contact a professional to sort out any legal disparities.

   - **Quitclaim Deeds:** *In the end, let's imagine that the grantor is unsure about the title of the property or doesn't want to be liable for any legal activity after they have transferred the title to the next person. So, they opt for a quitclaim deed.*

     In this type of deed, no covenants or warranties are made. And this depends on one's reputation. If they are a credible person then it is understandable. If they have a history of debauchery, fraud, or deceit, then one should be aware of the deed, and you might not want your clients to head that.

Also, any information you convey to your clients should form goodwill and their best interest, and should not be based on your conflict of interests.

3. **Essential elements of deeds:** *There are four components that a deed should carry at all costs as it is required by the law.*

- **Legality** *of the language*

- *A* **detailed and legal description** *of the property*

- **Name** *of the parties involved*

- **Signature of the grantor**

In the end, all deeds can be adjoined by liens, conveyances, or any additional information that adds to the legality and credibility of the transfer of title.

4. **Importance of Recording:** *For a deed to stand legal, it should be notified and recorded by the public notary or municipal office. The idea is to make the transfer public so if there are any legal claims, they should immediately be filed, or to just notify people that who is now the owner of the people. It is essential for the chain of titles, all designed for the best interest of the grantee, who can be an heir, buyer, investor, or any other party.*

And that's it!

We now know what deeds are and their essential elements. Let's now move on to seeing the tax aspects of the deeds.

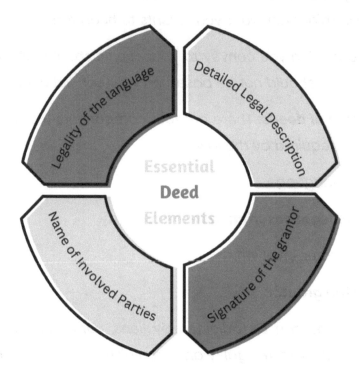

C. Escrow or Closing | The Tax Aspects of Transfers

Up till now, we know that if there are transfers to be made or any type of transaction, we have to pay tax. So, how can we skip the tax aspects when it comes to escrow accounts or closing the deal?

These aspects are crucial to understand for everyone regardless of who they are, or whether they are trying to just pass their PSI real estate exam.

Below mentioned are a few aspects that we want you to keep in mind:

1. *Responsibilities of Escrow Agents: As a real estate agent, it will be your responsibility to see and manage affairs related to escrow accounts. Your common obligations can include:*

- *Collecting and holding earnest money which can be a safe deposit to solidify trust in the agreement or deal. Collecting it from the buyer and doing it however, the owner wants you to do.*

- *An escrow agent is the one who can expect to be taking care of all the legal and tax documents, preparing other documents related to deeds and titles so that when the day of transfer arrives, there are no shortcomings.*

- *Also, as an escrow agent, you can expect to do home inspections, and other surveys to explore the validity of titles, and analyze the quality of the house, and the cost of renovations (if needed and depending on the underlying case scenario).*

A simple exercise

"Imagine a buyer calls you that the method of financing their purchase does not exist anymore, that they don't have the money, telling you all so at the last minute.

How will you mitigate and react in this situation to ensure the interest of all parties including the deal itself are protected?"

Here's out take on it:

For mitigation:

- *Explore alternative financing options such as private lending or seller financing.*

- *Negotiate an extension with the seller to allow time for the buyer to secure new financing.*

- *Offer to assist the buyer in finding alternative solutions, such as seeking out other lenders or financial advisors.*

Regarding reaction:

- *Remain calm and professional while reassuring all parties involved.*

- *Communicate transparently with both the buyer and seller about the situation and potential solutions.*

- *Document all communications and agreements to protect the interests of all parties and the integrity of the deal.*

2. **Prorated Items:** *Any payments or financial liabilities associated with a property that is to be divided among both parties (seller and buyer) can be referred to as prorated items. You will understand them once we mention some case scenarios related to prorated items:*

   - *Oftentimes, **property taxes** are agreed to be prorated between two parties, some might agree to pay taxes for the first half of the year, and the other to take care of the latter half.*

   - *Sometimes, any unpaid **utility bills** can also be prorated as to who will be responsible for which bill or any liability payments associated with the property.*

   - *In the end, there can be some **homeowner association (HOA)** fees that can be also agreed upon as to which party will be responsible for taking care of it, typically the buyer has to take care of it for the remaining time duration in which they own the property.*

3. **Closing Statements/TRID:** *Closing statements refer to a detailed description of all the payments or any fees that can be associated or required with the transfer of title. On the other hand, TRID is an amalgam of the "Truth in Lending Act" (TILA) and RESPA Integrated Disclosures. So, "T" in TRID represents TILA, while "RID" stands for RESPA Integrated Disclosures.*

   It's an important law that must be remembered by all of the agents. Some examples are as follows:

   - **CD:** *Closing disclosure form is a 5-page document indicating the final agreed terms and conditions of an agreement or a mortgage loan.*

   - **HUD-1 Settlement Statement:** *It's a form where a list of all charges that are to be paid by involved parties are listed.*

- **ALTA Settlement Statement:** *It's a form that is similar to the HUD-1. It is often used in its replacement. This form is administered by the American Land Title Association (ALTA).*

An Activity

"Create a sample CD or ALTA settlement statement form and take a look at all the essential elements such as closing costs or escrow details. You can include the following elements in the form:

1. **Property Information:** *Description of the property being transferred, including address, legal description, and parcel identification number.*

2. **Buyer and Seller Information:** *Names and contact information of the buyer(s) and seller(s), along with their respective agents or representatives.*

3. **Purchase Price and Financing Details:** *Total purchase price of the property, including any adjustments or prorations. Breakdown of financing, including loan amount, interest rate, and lender information.*

4. **Closing Costs:** *Itemized list of closing costs incurred by the buyer, seller, or both parties. Common closing costs may include loan origination fees, appraisal fees, title search fees, attorney fees, recording fees, and transfer taxes.*

5. **Escrow Details:** *Escrow account information, including the initial deposit, adjustments, and any remaining funds. Explanation of how escrow funds will be used to cover expenses such as property taxes, insurance premiums, and prepaid interest.*

6. **Prorations:** *Prorated expenses or credits associated with property taxes, homeowners' association dues, utilities, and other recurring charges.*

7. **Title Insurance:** *Disclosure of title insurance premiums and related fees, including owner's title insurance and lender's title insurance. Explanation of coverage and potential exceptions or exclusions.*

8. **Loan Disclosures:** *Disclosure of loan terms, including the total loan amount, interest rate, monthly payment, and any prepayment penalties or adjustable-rate provisions.*

9. **Any Additional Disclosures:** *Any additional disclosures required by state or federal regulations, such as the Real Estate Settlement Procedures Act (RESPA) or Truth in Lending Act (TILA).*

10. **Signatures:** *In the end, signatures of the buyer(s), seller(s), and closing agent or settlement agent, acknowledging receipt and understanding of the settlement statement.*

4. **Estimating Closing Costs:** *For a real estate agent to calculate closing costs is a discerning trait, one that helps them gain reputation and trust from their clients. These are some factors that you can consider while doing so to get a discreet closing statement:*

   - *Costs related to the lending process such as a lending fee charged by a lender for processing the loan application.*

   - *Costs that are associated with* **Title Insurance.**

   - *Costs charged by an attorney as sometimes you or your client might want to have a professional attorney take a look at your closing statement so that there are no disputes related to the agreement.*

5. **Property & Income Tax:** *Under the IRS and different state policies, everyone is entitled to pay property taxes based on their value and income (if any). Mostly, these are prorated between the two parties such as:*

   - *Property taxes are prorated between buyer and seller. Mostly, 50-50 distribution.*

   - *In case a seller sells a property, they are liable to the capital gains tax in case they make any profits from the sale. This capital gains tax depends on different factors such as how long the seller owned the property, and their tax status.*

In the end, calculating property taxes can get complex as they are dependent on a number of factors, and can be different from case to case. There are a couple of special processes that one must not forget in seeing the tax application of a property.

D. Special Processes

There are a couple of special processes that you need to be aware of as they act as fundamental engines powering the desirability of the deal or property.

1. ***Foreclosures:*** *It's a process of reclaiming property from a buyer who has defaulted on their mortgage loan. It begins when a borrower fails to pay monthly payments consecutively and it ends when the property gets claimed back by the lender, or the property gets sold at an auction. The auction is the last resort of a lender and they can be expected to provide a few opportunities for the defaulter to reinitiate their payment plan. And in case the property fails to get sold at an auction, it becomes REO (real estate owned) by the lender. They may choose to sell it later at a lower price through an agent/agency or auction once again!*

2. ***Short Sale:*** *These occur when a distressed homeowner requests a short sale of their property at an agreed price from the lender. This sale occurs at lesser a price than a mortgage payment owed by the owner. Now, if the remaining payable payments are less, the owner can expect to get them waived off, only if the lender approves the selling of the property in the first place. Lenders need to see the following factors while doing so:*

   - *Sellers should give a justifiable reason or prove any hardship to sell the property (seller qualification)*

   - *No short sale can start without the approval of the lender.*

   - *No short sale can occur without the homeowner sharing the purchase statements submitted to them with the lender. And their approval of whom you are selling to is necessary in this regard.*

An Activity

"Analyze a case study of a short sale transaction and identify the key steps involved in the process, including seller qualification, lender approval, and purchase offer submission."

E. Warranties

Why do we all want to own a property?

Why do homeowners buy?

It's simple!

To enjoy the peace and quality of life. Now, we know that life can be uncertain and there can be some calamities, so how best to ensure that same peace in our day-to-day life?

Well, by getting a warranty. Let's take a look at what purpose these fulfill in alignment with the scope of these factors for home and construction-related defects or issues:

1. ***Purpose of Home & Construction Warranty programs:*** *The purpose is simple here: to make sure that the homeowners get the best and most peaceful experience in owning a property, without having to worry about the defects and their coverage costs. It offers:*

    - *Mental Peace*

    - *Long-term reliability*

    - *Quality assurance*

    - *Consumer protections*

2. ***Scope of Home & Construction Warranty Programs:*** *There are a few reasons one might be looking to find a safe side under these warranty programs, especially when one discovers:*

    - *System defects such as quality issues with wiring or conductors, or HVAC-related issues.*

- *Structural issues such as roofing issues or any problem surfacing because of the poor quality material usage. In case, a real estate developer does that, this warranty program will protect you.*

- *Workmanship defects such as unskillful staff or poor installation*

  A common example would be a scenario in which a family purchases a newly constructed home. They opt for a home warranty program that covers structural defects, mechanical systems, and workmanship for a period of ten years. Several months after moving in, they discover a leak in the roof. Thanks to the warranty program, the repair costs are covered, sparing the family from significant financial strain."

So, these were all the important aspects and factors and types that are involved in the transfer of title. It is important to not overlook and possibly revise things related to titles and defects in your professional career. It's because you can try so hard to make sure that nothing goes wrong, but still, there is a likelihood that you miss out on some important thing or detail in the transfer phase of a real property.

Talking about practices, how about we discuss this in detail?

Exercise Questions

1. Differentiate between marketable and insurable titles, including their significance in real estate transactions.

2. Discuss why recording a deed is important in real estate transactions.

3. Describe the purpose of closing statements and TRID disclosures in real estate transactions.

4. Explain the scope of coverage provided by home or construction warranty programs.

Chapter 10

PRACTICE OF REAL ESTATE

The practice of real estate refers to the inbound principle that refers to the overall process of your activities and responsibilities. Up till now, we have discussed in detail different responsibilities or problems that you might be facing (imaginative).

Now, it is time for us to sort of revise the general practice, all that we have learned, along with some new concepts. All so that when you enter your PSI real estate exam, you have a memorized process in your head, which will make it easier for you to answer. Let's start once again from discussing the escrow accounts once again. We will try our best not to reinforce any previously discussed information.

A. Trust/Escrow Accounts

Throughout this book, in different chapters, we have had some mentions of escrow accounts. It's simply a safe deposit to show one's commitment to the deal.

Let's jump straight into exploring trust or escrow accounts.

1. *Purpose & Definition:* Trust or escrow accounts are simply accounts that are made by real estate agents, agencies, non-agencies, or attorneys to hold funds and money during the process of a deal transaction, or an agreement. As it sounds, it's a trust account where the agency or attorney takes 100% responsibility for the funds to be used however the depositor wants it to be. Also, in case of no progress, the depositor can claim back their money which the escrow account beholder is legally bound to do so.

2. ***Responsibilities for Trust Monies:*** *As a real estate professional, you will be required to take full responsibility for the client's funds. Doing so while making sure that there is no inappropriate use of funds, especially for personal use or purchases. Also, a professional should maintain strict records with every entry of the usage of their money.*

Because the best you can have is not someone's wallet. Instead, to gain that reputation which might inspire them to give you a nice bonus since you were so true to them. But you shouldn't expect anything, and do your job, as a trustee honestly!

These are your fiduciary responsibilities, and you are bound to follow them. A wise piece of advice is, "These all are for your benefit".

For example, imagine a scenario where a real estate agent deposits trust money into their account. Doesn't it sound concerning? Even if they did so accidentally, aren't they liable to provide an explanation to the involved parties?

That's why one needs to be responsible because reputation, is prudent to have!

It will be easier for you to now comprehend where you can expect to be when you start professionally. We have discussed ADA and Fair Housing before, let's take one more look at it before we near the conclusion of your journey.

B. Federal Housing Laws & the ADA

Both of these laws are there to protect citizen's rights, the people of the state, against any set of discrimination against them. It can be racial or based on marital status, or it can be related to disabilities which the Americans with Disabilities Act (ADA) protects.

Below mentioned are some of the key components that we think are the most relatable to consider.

1. ***Protected Classes:*** *As per the Federal Housing laws, there exist certain protected classes whose rights cannot be violated when it comes to real business. These classes are protected on the basis of:*

- **Color or race**

- **Nationality**

- **Marital status**

- **Disability and so on.**

  As a real estate professional, it will be your duty to know these regulations first and then comply with them throughout your career. Again, for your best interest only!

2. **Prohibited Conduct:** *There are certain practices that are prohibited under the protective umbrella of these two laws. Some of the most common ones are:*

   - **Redlining:** *Real estate agents and professionals cannot redline requests from any specific location and their conduct should be fair instead of discriminatory.*

   - **Blockbusting:** *Real estate agents and agencies cannot spread false news to fuel their motives such as creating false hype about a property or a piece of false news that properties are going to crash, resulting in people rushing to sell their properties, only to discover later that it was a piece of false news and that properties price skyrocketed. It is a common fraud in the industry and you should avoid it. Because it's not about the money, it's about value. Sometimes, you cannot buy just value, no matter how rich you are!*

   - **Steering:** *It's when professionals drive customers away from a certain area or neighborhood.*

3. **Americans with Disabilities Act (ADA):** *We have already discussed this in detail. To avoid repeating ideas, please head back to "Section E" of Chapter 8.*

4. **Exemptions:** *There is always room for certain cases where exemptions can be seen. For if there is a small building with fewer or up to 4 units, the owner of that property might not be bound by federal housing or ADA laws. In cases like these, it is important to consult a real estate lawyer for a correct inquiry. As it will help you to avoid certain disputes in the future. In case you don't want to hire someone, then it's an even*

greater idea as it will empower your legal knowledge, interaction with legal language, and competitiveness.

Let's now take a look at another important face of the real estate world, one that we haven't discussed enough in this book.

C. Advertising & Technology

Throughout the contents of this PSI exam book, we have tried to address concepts and topics relating to the paperwork or general principles of the real estate industry. But there is another side that you need to know about.

The information that is coming ahead is necessary for you when you level up in your career, and where you now interact with developers. Also, in order to promote your agency and to make sure that it is seen by the targeted audience, you need to employ certain practices.

It's a key to a successful business.

1. ***Advertising Practices:*** *While advertising, the agency or whoever wants to promote their property service or product, there are certain practices that should be ensured at all costs such as:*

    a. ***Truth in Advertising:*** *As we have forever pressed the importance of truth and goodwill in the contents of this book, the same applies to advertising. When advertising, it is important that you should not add something from your own. Such as advertising a house with a large swimming pool or four bedrooms, when in reality, it has just a little tub and 2 bedrooms. Once again, all of these regulations and responsibilities are in your best interest.*

    b. ***Fair Housing Issues in Advertising:*** *Since the fair housing laws protect people from any discrimination, the same rules apply to advertisers. For example, if you are running your ad on the local TV or YouTube, then it should not contain any discriminatory words or imagery, or even jokes. Your goal is to interact instead of* repelling people. For example, you cannot express that a property is ideal for a young girl with a job. It is discriminatory!

2. **Use of Technology:** With technology, there come certain threats such as data leaks or any vital information that can affect the stature of an agent, agency, or client. It can include:

    a. **Requirements for Confidential Information:** In order to safeguard vital information and documents, it is important to adhere to strict protocols so that nothing goes wrong or ends up in the wrong hands. This can mean:

        - *Personal Data*

        - *Financial documents or records*

        - *Other confidential information that can affect the relationship or the agreement*

A short exercise!

"Develop a list outlining all the crucial steps that you think real estate agents should take to maintain compliance with confidentiality requirements when using technology in their practice."

    b. _Do-Not-Call List:_ _Agents and agencies are required by the regulations to keep a do-not-call list. This list includes people who were once contacted through the telemarketing calls but they requested not to be called again. When they say so, it is important to enter their details in the do-not-call list. And you should never call them again._

D. Licensee & Requirements

Now, when you start out your career professionally, there will be certain requirements that you will have to follow, depending on your role and position. It is necessary to understand that even though when you are a licensee (carrying a real estate agent license), you will be weighed by experience at the start, and then by your reputation.

So, when starting out, one should be willing to do whatever responsibilities are required of them. A few common cases are:

    a. _Employee:_ _This is most likely to be your start. When you get a job in a real estate firm or an agency, you become their employee, requiring you to take care of certain agreed tasks for the prosperity of the company you work in. It is the duty of the employer to provide you necessary guidance and information so you can do your job easily._

    b. _Independent Contractor:_ _This is the ideal start for people who are looking for long-term growth in the industry. Independent contractors can work with agencies and firms but they are more likely so the right to have more time and space, and better client relationships. For example, you are an independent contractor/agent affiliated with an agency or firm. You have the flexibility to set your own schedule, market yourself, and negotiate terms with clients. However,_ *you are also responsible for covering your expenses, such as marketing materials and insurance.*

c. ***Due Diligence for Real Estate Transactions:*** *Due diligence refers to the thorough process we have discussed a few times before in this book, one where we do our research related to property records, market value, and conditions, or any potential risks to the transaction. For example, if you have a job to conduct due diligence on a house, then you can expect to visit the site and look for any damages or defects that can affect the property value. Similarly, for a commercial building, you can check the authority of design and structure, zoning regulations, or if it is contributing to environmental waste or habitat loss.*

In the end, let's take a look at antitrust laws so you know the potential outcomes of one's wrongdoings or irresponsible behavior in the industry.

Antitrust Laws

These laws are there to protect citizens and all the parties involved in the real estate transaction from any mischief or defects that could potentially harm their reputation or performance in the years to come.

Let's take a look at important aspects of antitrust laws:

1. ***Antitrust Laws and Purpose:*** *These laws are there to make sure that fair competition exists in the market and that not one company or party has all the profits. It's to ensure that a market runs in an unbiased direction. The purpose is to constrict monopolistic behavior where a group of people can join hands together to manipulate the market for their best interests, which is a serious crime.*

2. ***Antitrust Violations in Real Estate:*** *Even though we have the law for everything, crimes still do occur, and violations are still made. Note that, these violations should not be taken lightly and that they can seriously bring one to justice, where they can get harsh penalties or punishments.*

Just like that, you now know all the essentials of being a real estate professional. We understand that it might have sounded difficult at the start. But it is only difficult in the imagination.

Now, we just need one more important chapter to discuss before we end our journey here. It is to level calculable skills.

Exercise Questions to Test Your Knowledge

1. List and briefly explain the protected classes under federal fair housing laws. Give an example of a situation where discrimination based on a protected class might occur.

2. What are the requirements for handling confidential information in real estate transactions? How does the Do-Not-Call List impact real estate marketing efforts?

Chapter 11

REAL ESTATE CALCULATIONS

I t is human psychology that we learn more of the formulas and from real experiences than thousands of books can do. To level up your calculation skills and your chances of passing the PSI real estate exam, we have some of the topics that are essential for you to memorize. You will need a lot of this in your real life.

A. Basic Math Concepts

Some of the basic math concepts that are so essential in the overall real estate journey are:

1. **Loan-to-Value Ratios (LTV):** *As explained before if you recall it, LTV is an important factor for lenders to consider before financing a loan to the homebuyer. This is how you calculate it:*

   LTV Ratio = (Loan Amount/Property Value) * 100

   Imagine a buyer is purchasing a property at $200,000 while he needs $160,000 from mortgage loan financing. His LTV ratio will be:

   LTV Ratio = ($160,000/$200,000) * 100

   LTV Ratio = **80%** *(which is fair but a tough one as it should not be higher than 80%)*

An Exercise

"Calculate the LTV ratio for a property valued at $300,000 with a mortgage loan amount of $230,000. Would they be able to secure it as per the 80% rule?"

(for solution, see chapter 12)

2. **Discount Points:** *It's a fee that you pay to a lender upfront on a mortgage loan at closing. One can do it because it helps reduce the interest rate on the mortgage loan. One point, mainly, represents 1% of the mortgage loan.*

   If one is smart with discount points, one can save some money. In the end, normally, payment of 1 point upfront can help reduce interest rates by .125 to .25% (it can vary and depends on a lot of factors). Its formula is:

   Total Cost of Discount Points = Amount of Loan x Number of Points / 100

   For example, If Adam is obtaining a mortgage loan of $200,000 and wants to pay 2 discount points, each valued at 1% of the loan amount, the total cost of discount points would be:

   Total Cost of Discount Points = $200,000 x 2 / 100

   Total Cost of Discount Points = $400,000 / 100

   Total Cost of Discount Points = $4,000

   That's what Adam saves if he pays 2 discount points upfront!

3. **Equity:** *It's simply a difference between property value and outstanding liens or mortgages against it. It is basically what an owner owns and this percentage tends to grow over time, as the owner will pay more and more of the monthly payments. It is calculated as:*

   Equity = Property Value – Outstanding balance

   For example, if a property is valued at $500,000 and the outstanding mortgage payment is $100,000, then the owner's equity or stake in the property would be:

   Equity = $500,000 - $100,000

   Equity = $400,000 *(which means that the owner has an 80% stake in the property)*

4. **Down Payment/Amount to be financed:** *Whatever we pay initially when buying a property is called down payment. And whatever that remains after that is called the amount to be financed.*

   To calculate the amount to be financed, let's take a look at this example:

   If a property is priced at $300,000, and the buyer makes a down payment of $40,000, then the amount to be financed would be:

   Amount to be Financed = *$300,000 - $40,000*

   Amount to be Financed = $260,000

A Simple Exercise

"Calculate the down payment and amount to be financed for a property priced at $500,000 with a down payment of 20%."

(For solution, check chapter 12)

B. Calculations for Transactions

There are some more mathematical calculations that can exist apart from these basic ones. These are more involved when the transaction stage is reached. You need to understand them as well.

Let's take a look at a few of the most important transaction calculations:

1. **Property Tax Calculations:** *As a responsible citizen of the state, it is the responsibility of every individual to pay property taxes and related taxes that are imposed by the government. These taxes are imposed based on the proposed or assessed value of the property. Also, the tax rate can vary so we tried designing a simple formula that will work with every tax bracket (you will need to research the state and tax information but in case of your exam, it will already be given):*

   Property Tax = Assessed Value x Tax Rate

For example, if a property is valued at $200,000 and the tax rate is 1.5%, the property tax would be:

Property Tax = $200,000 x 0.015 (1.5/100 = 0.015)

Property Tax = $3,000

A Simple Question!

"Calculate the annual property tax for a property assessed at $350,000 with a tax rate of 2%."

(For solution, see chapter 12)

2. **Prorations:** As discussed before, these are adjustments or agreeable terms of distributions of any liabilities, HOA fees, or taxes related to the property. These are signed between the buyer and the seller on the closing date. Also, it should mention the duration for which the certain person would be responsible.

   Proration = (Expense/No. of days in a year) x Number of days owed

   For example, if the annual property tax is $3,000, and the closing occurs 60 days into the year, the prorated property tax owed by the seller would be:

   Prorated Property Tax = ($3,000 / 365) x 60

   Prorated Property Tax = $492.74

A Simple Exercise

"Calculate the prorated property tax owed by the buyer if the closing occurs 120 days into the year for the same case scenario mentioned above."

3. **Commission & Commission Splits:** There is nothing in this world that doesn't have a price. The same applies to real estate agents and professionals as they charge for their services, all of which we have discussed above. Mathematically, commissions are easy to calculate. Before that, just know that commission splits mean as to who is responsible for the commission from whom. In some cases, an agent can charge both the seller and the buyer. The general formula for a commission is:

Commission = Sale Price × Agreed Commission Rate

For example, if a property sells for $300,000 with a commission rate of 6%, the total commission earned by the agent will be:

Commission = $300,000 x 6%

Commission = $300,000 x 6/100

Commission = $18,000

A Simple Exercise

"Calculate the commission earned by the buyer's agent for a property sold at $500,000 with a 3% commission rate, assuming a 50/50 split between the listing and buyer's agents."

(Solution in Chapter 12)

(A simple tip: divide the result by 2 since it's a 50/50 split).

4. **Seller's Proceeds of Sale:** It is important for sellers to take into account all the costs that we have mentioned such as taxes, commissions, or other fees. It is for their own benefit as they can then reach the target profit that they are looking for from a deal.

   So, seller proceeds are the net amount that the owner will have from a sale of the property, after deducting all of the expenses.

   It can be calculated as:

   Seller's Proceeds = Sale Price – (agent's commission + other costs)

   Using the above formula, try to calculate this question using your common sense:

   "If a property sells for $400,000, and the seller pays a 5% commission to the real estate agent, with extra closing costs of $10,000, what are the seller's proceeds of sale?"

   (Solution in chapter 12)

5. **Buyer Funds Needed at Closing:** *Similar to the seller's proceeds, buyers also need to consider the commission paid to the agent, property taxes in case proration occurs, and other costs to calculate what is the actual price that they are paying for the property. It can be calculated as:*

Buyer Funds Needed = Down Payment + Closing Costs

Another question for you, "If a buyer is buying a property for $650,000 and is required to make a 20% down payment, with closing costs totaling $10,000, how much funds does the buyer need at closing?"

Start by first calculating the down payment and then it will be easier from there. (solution in chapter 12)

6. **Transfer Fees/Conveyance Tax/Revenue Stamps:** *These are charges that are imposed by the government mostly when the transfer is being made at the local, municipal, or state level. As an agent, you need to consider these fees as well to get a reasonable target estimate of the total amount required by your client to buy or sell a property. In case of complex scenarios, you should not hesitate to contact a real estate lawyer. Because mostly you will have to do this, agencies have these lawyers on their teams, as everyone in this world of estates needs them.*

7. **PITI:** *This stands for Principal, Interest, Taxes, and Insurance. It is basically a measure of most of the liable payments that come with a property, that one has to pay. In order to find the PITI amount, you just need to add all of them up.*

PITI = Principal + Interest + Taxes + Insurance

Now, A question for you, "if a homeowner's monthly mortgage payment includes $1,200 in principal, $800 in interest, $300 in property taxes, and $100 in homeowner's insurance, what is the total PITI payment?"

(solution in chapter 12)

In the end, for a detailed description of PITI, please refer to "Chapter 4 – Section A – 5".

And that's it. These were some of the calculations that you should know on a day-to-day scale. *Note that, sometimes things will not be as easy to calculate as they appear here in the formulas. Some information might be missing. In those cases, your duty is to try to provide an accurate figure or calculation results to your client. In case you are unable to, you can just ask a professional.*

Chapter 12

PRACTICE EXAM ⊠ QUESTIONS & ANSWERS

Below mentioned are some questions in the same order as the outline of this book. The answers are given after the questions!

1. Which of the following is an example of real property?

A) Car

B) Boat

C) House

D) Jewelry

2. What is the purpose of legal descriptions in real estate?

A) To describe personal property

B) To establish property taxes

C) To define the boundaries of real property

D) To determine rental rates

3. Which legal description method uses compass directions and distances to define property boundaries?

A) Lot and block

B) Government survey system

C) Metes and bounds

D) Rectangular survey system

4. What type of rights include the right to extract resources such as oil or minerals from the land?

A) Water rights

B) Air rights

C) Mineral rights

D) Easement rights

5. What is an example of an encumbrance on a property?

A) Deed

C) Easement

B) Mortgage

D) Warranty

6. What type of ownership involves ownership by two or more individuals with no right of survivorship?

A) Joint tenancy

C) Tenancy in common

B) Tenancy by the entirety

D) Community property

7. Which type of ownership involves shared ownership of a property with a specified time period?

A) Tenancy in common

C) Timeshare

B) Joint tenancy

D) Condominium

8. What type of encroachment involves a neighbor's fence extending onto your property?

A) Easement

C) Encumbrance

B) Lien

D) Encroachment

9. Which type of ownership involves ownership by one individual or entity?

A) Joint tenancy

C) Ownership in severalty

B) Tenancy by the entirety

D) Tenancy in common

10. What is the purpose of a life estate ownership?

A) Ownership by two or more individuals

C) Ownership for the lifetime of the owner or another designated person

B) Ownership by a single individual for a specified period

D) Ownership with rights of survivorship

11. **Which type of ownership includes rights of survivorship?**

A) Tenants in common

C) Tenancy by the entirety

B) Joint tenancy

D) Ownership in severalty

12. **What is a common type of encumbrance that provides security for a debt?**

A) Easement

C) Covenant

B) Lien

D) Deed restriction

13. **Which type of ownership involves shared ownership of a property with common areas and joint ownership of individual units?**

A) Timeshare

C) Condominium

B) Cooperative

D) Tenancy in common

14. **What is the purpose of the rectangular government survey system (RGSS)?**

A) To describe property using metes and bounds

C) To establish property taxes

B) To divide land into townships and sections

D) To determine rental rates

15. **Which term refers to the area of a property that is suitable for living or rental purposes?**

A) Livable area

C) Usable area

B) Rentable area

D) Total area

16. **What type of ownership involves shared ownership of a property with joint ownership of the land and buildings?**

A) Condominium

C) Timeshare

B) Cooperative

D) Joint tenancy

17. Which type of legal description method divides land into townships, ranges, and sections?

A) Metes and bounds

B) Lot and block

C) Government survey system

D) Rectangular survey system

18. What is the purpose of an easement?

A) To transfer ownership of property

B) To provide security for a debt

C) To restrict the use of property

D) To grant limited use of property to another party

19. Which type of encumbrance involves a claim on a property as security for a debt?

A) Lien

B) Easement

C) Covenant

D) Deed restriction

20. Which type of ownership involves ownership by a married couple with rights of survivorship?

A) Joint tenancy

B) Tenancy in common

C) Tenancy by the entirety

D) Community property

21. Which of the following is NOT a government right in land?

A) Property taxes

B) Eminent domain

C) Easement

D) Escheat

22. What is the process by which the government takes private property for public use, with just compensation to the property owner?

A) Adverse possession

B) Eminent domain

C) Condemnation

D) Escheat

23. Which of the following is an example of a private control over land use?

A) Zoning ordinances

B) Building codes

C) Deed restrictions

D) Eminent domain

24. Which government control regulates the use of land in specific geographical areas to ensure orderly development and protect property values?

A) Building codes

B) Zoning ordinances

C) Eminent domain

D) Easements

25. What is the term for the process by which government acquires private property for public use?

A) Easement

B) Condemnation

C) Escheat

D) Deed restriction

26. Flood zones and wetlands are examples of:

A) Zoning regulations

B) Building codes

C) Environmental hazards

D) Deed restrictions

27. Which of the following is NOT a type of environmental hazard?

A) Lead contamination

B) Radon gas

C) Zoning regulations

D) Asbestos

28. What is the term for a legal document that restricts the use of property?

A) Zoning ordinance

B) Building code

C) Easement

D) Deed restriction

29. What is the purpose of building codes?

A) To regulate property taxes

B) To ensure public safety and welfare

C) To establish zoning districts

D) To control environmental hazards

30. Which government control determines how land can be used within designated zones?

A) Building codes

B) Deed restrictions

C) Zoning ordinances

D) Eminent domain

31. What is the term for the right of government to take private property for public use?

A) Easement

B) Escheat

C) Eminent domain

D) Condemnation

32. Which of the following is an example of a private control over land use?

A) Zoning ordinance

B) Eminent domain

C) Deed restriction

D) Condemnation

33. What is the process by which the government regulates the use of land to protect public health, safety, and welfare?

A) Zoning

B) Eminent domain

C) Condemnation

D) Escheat

34. Which of the following is a government control over land use?

A) Easement

B) Deed restriction

C) Zoning ordinance

D) Covenant

35. What type of land use control regulates the size, height, and use of buildings within specified areas?

A) Deed restrictions

B) Building codes

C) Zoning ordinances

D) Easements

36. What is the term for a legal restriction on the use of real property, usually imposed by the seller when the property is conveyed?

A) Eminent domain

C) Deed restriction

B) Zoning ordinance

D) Easement

37. Which of the following is NOT a form of private control over land use?

A) Easement

C) Deed restriction

B) Covenant

D) Zoning ordinance

38. What is the term for the process by which government regulates the use of land and structures within designated areas?

A) Eminent domain

C) Deed restriction

B) Zoning

D) Easement

39. Which of the following is a government control over land use?

A) Covenant

C) Zoning ordinance

B) Easement

D) Deed restriction

40. What type of government control regulates the use of land to prevent incompatible uses in specific areas?

A) Zoning

C) Escheat

B) Condemnation

D) Eminent domain

41. What is the primary purpose of real estate appraisals?

A) To determine property taxes

C) To establish rental rates

B) To estimate the market value of a property

D) To assess homeowner's insurance

42. Which of the following is NOT a general step in the appraisal process?

A) Property inspection

B) Data analysis

C) Property marketing

D) Value reconciliation

43. In which situation would a property typically require an appraisal by a certified appraiser?

A) When applying for a building permit

B) When refinancing a mortgage

C) When hiring a property manager

D) When hiring a landscaper

44. Which economic principle suggests that the value of a property is influenced by its proximity to amenities and services?

A) Supply and demand

B) Substitution

C) Conformity

D) Location

45. Which approach to estimating value relies on the principle of substitution?

A) Sales or market comparison approach

B) Cost approach

C) Income analysis approach

D) Gross Rent Multipliers (GRM)

46. What is the primary focus of the cost approach to estimating value?

A) Estimating potential rental income

B) Determining the property's resale value

C) Calculating the cost to replace the property

D) Analyzing historical sales data

47. Which approach to estimating value is commonly used for valuing income-producing properties such as apartment buildings?

A) Cost approach

B) Income analysis approach

C) Sales or market comparison approach

D) Gross Income Multipliers (GIM)

48. What does GRM stand for in real estate valuation?

A) Gross Rental Margin

B) Gross Rent Multiplier

C) Gross Revenue Model

D) Gross Return Method

49. How is Gross Income Multiplier (GIM) calculated?

A) Gross Income ÷ Gross Expenses

B) Gross Income ÷ Property Value

C) Net Income ÷ Property Value

D) Net Income ÷ Gross Expenses

50. Which of the following is NOT a factor typically considered in the sales or market comparison approach?

A) Location

B) Age of the property

C) Replacement cost

D) Size of the property

51. When would the cost approach to estimating value be most appropriate?

A) For new construction properties

B) For historic properties with unique features

C) For income-producing properties

D) For properties with high rental demand

52. Which approach to estimating value is based on the principle of capitalization?

A) Sales or market comparison approach

B) Cost approach

C) Income analysis approach

D) Gross Rent Multipliers (GRM)

53. In the income analysis approach, what does the term "capitalization rate" refer to?

A) The rate at which property values depreciate over time

B) The rate of return an investor expects from the property

C) The rate of inflation applied to rental income

D) The rate at which rental rates increase annually

54. Which of the following is true regarding the Gross Rent Multiplier (GRM)?

A) It considers only the gross rental income of a property.

B) It is calculated by dividing the net operating income by the property value.

C) It is primarily used for single-family residential properties.

D) It ignores rental income altogether.

55. What property characteristic does the cost approach primarily rely on?

A) Rental income potential

B) Market demand

C) Physical condition

D) Proximity to amenities

56. Which approach to estimating value is most commonly used by appraisers?

A) Sales or market comparison approach

B) Cost approach

C) Income analysis approach

D) Gross Income Multipliers (GIM)

57. What does the Gross Income Multiplier (GIM) indicate about a property?

A) Its potential for rental income

B) Its overall market value

C) Its age and condition

D) Its operating expenses

58. What does the term "comparables" refer to in the sales or market comparison approach?

A) Properties with similar characteristics that are used to estimate the value of a subject property

B) Properties with significant differences that are used to estimate the value of a subject property

C) Properties that are currently listed for sale

D) Properties that have been foreclosed

59. Which approach to estimating value is most commonly used for vacant land?

A) Cost approach

C) Sales or market comparison approach

B) Income analysis approach

D) Gross Income Multipliers (GIM)

60. What principle does the income analysis approach rely on to estimate value?

A) Substitution

C) Capitalization

B) Supply and demand

D) Highest and best use

61. What does "LTV" stand for in real estate financing?

A) Landlord Tenant Value

C) Loan Term Variation

B) Loan to Value

D) Loan Title Verification

62. What does "PMI" refer to in real estate financing?

A) Property Management Inspection

C) Property Maintenance Information

B) Private Mortgage Insurance

D) Payment Management Invoice

63. Which of the following is included in PITI?

A) Property Insurance, Title Insurance, Taxes, Interest

C) Property Inspection, Title Insurance, Taxes, Interest

B) Principal, Interest, Taxes, Insurance

D) Principal, Interest, Title Insurance, Insurance

64. What is the term for the amount charged by a lender to a borrower for the use of money?

A) Rent

C) Interest

B) Principal

D) Mortgage

65. What is the abbreviation "PITI" commonly used to represent in real estate financing?

A) Prepaid Interest and Taxes Information

B) Property Inspection and Title Information

C) Principal, Interest, Taxes, and Insurance

D) Property Investment and Trustee Information

66. Which of the following is an example of a financing instrument?

A) Title Insurance

B) Property Appraisal

C) Mortgage

D) Home Inspection

67. Which type of loan is insured by the Federal Housing Administration (FHA)?

A) Conventional Loan

B) VA Guaranteed Loan

C) FHA Insured Loan

D) Bridge Loan

68. What is the main characteristic of an amortized loan?

A) The interest rate remains fixed for the entire term of the loan

B) The loan balance decreases over time through regular payments

C) The loan balance increases over time due to interest accrual

D) The loan is paid off in a single lump sum payment at the end of the term

69. What is a feature of an adjustable-rate mortgage (ARM) loan?

A) The interest rate remains fixed for the entire term of the loan

B) The interest rate adjusts periodically based on market conditions

C) The borrower is not required to make monthly payments

D) The loan balance increases over time due to interest accrual

70. In owner financing, what is a "land contract" also known as?

A) Deed of Trust

B) Mortgage Note

C) Contract for Deed

D) Promissory Note

71. **What is the process of evaluating a borrower's financial situation and the risk associated with granting a loan called?**

A) Appraisal

B) Inspection

C) Underwriting

D) Escrow

72. Which law requires lenders to disclose the terms and costs of a mortgage loan?

A) Real Estate Settlement Procedures Act (RESPA)

B) Truth in Lending Act (TILA)

C) Equal Credit Opportunity Act (ECOA)

D) Consumer Financial Protection Bureau (CFPB)

73. What does RESPA stand for?

A) Real Estate Sales and Purchase Act

B) Real Estate Settlement Procedures Act

C) Residential Property Sales Agreement

D) Real Estate Services and Pricing Agreement

74. Which of the following laws prohibits discrimination in lending based on race, color, religion, national origin, sex, marital status, age, or receipt of income from public assistance programs?

A) Truth in Lending Act (TILA)

B) Real Estate Settlement Procedures Act (RESPA)

C) Equal Credit Opportunity Act (ECOA)

D) Consumer Financial Protection Bureau (CFPB)

75. What is one of the factors considered during underwriting of a loan?

A) Property size

B) Debt ratios

C) Property location

D) Credit card limit

76. What is the purpose of the Truth in Lending Act (TILA)?

A) To regulate the real estate appraisal process

B) To ensure fair and accurate credit reporting

C) To protect consumers by requiring clear disclosure of loan terms and costs

D) To establish guidelines for property tax assessments

77. What does CFPB/TRID stand for regarding real estate financing?

A) Consumer Financial Protection Bureau/Taxation Rules for Interest and Deductions

B) Credit Fairness Protection Bureau/Title Insurance and Disclosure

C) Consumer Finance Protection Bureau/TILA-RESPA Integrated Disclosures

D) Credit Fraud Prevention Bureau/Transfer of Real Estate Information and Documentation

78. What is the primary purpose of the Real Estate Settlement Procedures Act (RESPA)?

A) To regulate the sale of real estate properties

B) To prevent fraudulent real estate practices

C) To provide consumers with information about closing costs and eliminate kickbacks

D) To establish guidelines for property appraisals

79. Which of the following is NOT a factor typically considered during the underwriting process for a loan?

A) Employment history

B) Credit scoring

C) Vehicle ownership

D) Debt-to-income ratio

80. What does "LTV" represent in the context of loan underwriting?

A) Loan to Value

C) Lender Title Variation

B) Loan Term Verification

D) Loan Tracking Value

81. What is a common requirement for borrowers applying for a mortgage loan?

A) Must have a minimum credit score of 800

C) Must own multiple properties

B) Must have a steady income source

D) Must be a citizen of a foreign country

82. Which of the following is an example of a risky loan feature regulated by the CFPB/TRID rules?

A) Fixed interest rate

C) Amortization schedule

B) Balloon payment

D) Low debt-to-income ratio

83. What is the maximum allowable debt-to-income ratio for most conventional loans?

A) 20%

C) 36%

B) 30%

D) 50%

84. Which law prohibits lenders from discriminating against borrowers based on race, color, religion, sex, national origin, age, or marital status?

A) Fair Housing Act

C) Equal Credit Opportunity Act

B) Truth in Lending Act

D) Real Estate Settlement Procedures Act

85. What is the purpose of credit scoring in the lending process?

A) To determine the borrower's employment history

C) To calculate the loan-to-value ratio

B) To assess the borrower's creditworthiness based on their credit history

D) To verify the borrower's income

86. What is the primary role of the Consumer Financial Protection Bureau (CFPB) in relation to real estate financing?

A) To provide loans to consumers

B) To regulate financial institutions and protect consumers in the financial marketplace

C) To set interest rates for mortgage loans

D) To oversee property appraisals

87. Which law requires lenders to provide borrowers with a Loan Estimate and Closing Disclosure?

A) Truth in Lending Act (TILA)

B) Real Estate Settlement Procedures Act (RESPA)

C) Equal Credit Opportunity Act (ECOA)

D) Consumer Financial Protection Act (CFPA)

88. What is the primary purpose of a bridge loan in real estate financing?

A) To finance the purchase of a new primary residence

B) To provide temporary financing until permanent financing can be arranged

C) To finance the construction of a new commercial property

D) To refinance an existing mortgage at a lower interest rate

89. What is one of the key factors considered by lenders during the underwriting process?

A) Property value

B) Monthly utility bills

C) Number of bedrooms in the property

D) Personal hobbies of the borrower

90. What does "CFPB" stand for in the context of real estate financing?

A) Consumer Fraud Prevention Bureau

B) Credit Fairness Protection Bureau

C) Consumer Financial Protection Bureau

D) Certified Financial Planning Board

91. What type of relationship does a facilitator typically have with clients in a real estate transaction?

A) Fiduciary

B) Transactional

C) Non-agent

D) Dual agency

92. Which of the following is NOT a traditional agency duty?

A) Confidentiality

B) Disclosure

C) Accountability

D) Loyalty

93. What is a key element of a buyer brokerage/tenant representation contract?

A) Confidentiality clause

B) Duties of the agent

C) Price negotiation terms

D) Property disclosure requirements

94. When does an agency agreement typically expire?

A) Upon completion of the transaction

B) When the property is destroyed

C) Upon mutual agreement

D) After a specified period of time

95. What type of agency duty involves acting in the best interests of the client?

A) Confidentiality

B) Loyalty

C) Disclosure

D) Obedience

96. Which type of relationship does a real estate facilitator typically have with customers?

A) Fiduciary

B) Transactional

C) Dual agency

D) Principal-agent

97. In which situation would an agency agreement typically be terminated by force of law?

A) Mutual agreement

B) Destruction of property

C) Death of the principal

D) Bankruptcy of the agent

98. What is the primary responsibility of an agent to customers and third parties?

A) Loyalty

B) Honesty

C) Disclosure

D) Obedience

99. What type of agency relationship involves a real estate agent representing both the buyer and seller in a transaction?

A) Facilitator

B) Non-agent

C) Dual agency

D) Transactional

100. Which duty requires an agent to keep client information confidential?

A) Obedience

B) Disclosure

C) Confidentiality

D) Honesty

101. What is a key element of different types of listing contracts?

A) Price negotiation terms

B) Duties of the agent

C) Property disclosure requirements

D) Commission structure

102. When does an agency agreement terminate upon completion/performance?

A) Upon the expiration of the specified term

B) When the agent dies

C) When the property is destroyed

D) Upon mutual agreement

103. In which situation would an agency agreement typically terminate due to the destruction of property?

A) Mutual agreement

B) Death of the principal

C) Completion of the transaction

D) When the property is destroyed

104. What is a fiduciary responsibility of an agent to their client?

A) Loyalty

B) Honesty

C) Disclosure

D) Accountability

105. What type of relationship does a real estate agent have with clients when acting as a principal in a transaction?

A) Fiduciary

B) Dual agency

C) Non-agent

D) Principal-agent

106. What duty requires an agent to provide accurate and complete information to clients and third parties?

A) Honesty

B) Confidentiality

C) Disclosure

D) Loyalty

107. When does an agency agreement typically terminate due to the death of the principal?

A) Upon mutual agreement

B) Completion of the transaction

C) When the property is destroyed

D) Death of the principal

108. What is the responsibility of an agent to disclose conflicts of interest?

A) Obedience

B) Disclosure

C) Loyalty

D) Honesty

109. What type of agent relationship involves representing neither the buyer nor the seller in a transaction?

A) Facilitator

B) Dual agency

C) Transactional

D) Non-agent

110. In which situation would an agency agreement typically terminate upon mutual agreement?

A) When the property is destroyed

B) Expiration of the specified term

C) Bankruptcy of the agent

D) Mutual agreement

111. **What is a traditional agency duty that requires an agent to follow the lawful instructions of their client?**

A) Loyalty

B) Disclosure

C) Obedience

D) Confidentiality

112. **When does an agency agreement typically terminate due to the completion of the transaction?**

A) Upon expiration of the specified term

B) Mutual agreement

C) When the property is destroyed

D) Completion of the transaction

113. **What type of agent relationship involves representing both the buyer and seller as clients in the same transaction?**

A) Facilitator

B) Non-agent

C) Dual agency

D) Transactional

114. **What is the primary responsibility of an agent to customers and third parties?**

A) Loyalty

B) Disclosure

C) Honesty

D) Accountability

115. **What type of agent relationship involves representing neither the buyer nor the seller in a transaction?**

A) Facilitator

B) Non-agent

C) Dual agency

D) Principal-agent

116. **What type of agent relationship involves representing both the buyer and seller in a transaction?**

A) Facilitator

B) Non-agent

C) Dual agency

D) Transactional

117. **What duty requires an agent to keep client information confidential?**

A) Obedience

B) Disclosure

C) Confidentiality

D) Honesty

118. **What is a key element of different types of listing contracts?**

A) Price negotiation terms

B) Duties of the agent

C) Property disclosure requirements

D) Commission structure

119. **What duty requires an agent to provide accurate and complete information to clients and third parties?**

A) Honesty

B) Confidentiality

C) Disclosure

D) Loyalty

120. **What type of agent relationship involves representing neither the buyer nor the seller in a transaction?**

A) Facilitator

B) Dual agency

C) Transactional

D) Non-agent

121. **Which of the following property conditions may warrant inspections and surveys?**

A) Fresh coat of paint

B) New landscaping

C) Suspected mold growth

D) Upgraded kitchen appliances

122. **When should inquiries about public or private land use controls be made?**

A) When the property has a well-maintained garden

B) When the property is located in a gated community

C) When proposed uses or changes in uses are anticipated

D) When there's a high demand for rental properties in the area

123. **Which environmental issue typically requires disclosure?**

A) High property taxes

B) Presence of asbestos

C) Recent property upgrades

D) Nearby shopping centers

124. **What does LEAD stand for in government disclosure requirements?**

A) Land Engineering and Development

B) Legal Entity Assessment Division

C) Lead-based paint disclosure

D) Local Environmental Agency Directive

125. **What type of information should be disclosed regarding material facts and defects?**

A) Only information the seller feels comfortable disclosing

B) Any information that might impact the property's value or desirability

C) Information that favors the seller's interests

D) Information related to recent renovations

126. **In the context of property condition, which of the following would typically warrant an inspection?**

A) Routine cleaning of the property

B) A leaking roof

C) Basic landscaping maintenance

D) Replacing light bulbs in the house

127. **Which of the following would NOT trigger inquiries about land use controls?**

A) An application for rezoning in the neighborhood

B) Construction of a new playground nearby

C) Plans for a high-rise building on adjacent property

D) A recent increase in property taxes

128. **What environmental issue should be disclosed to potential buyers?**

A) A recent termite inspection

B) Presence of lead-based paint

C) Property boundary disputes

D) A new HVAC system installation

129. Under government disclosure requirements, what must be disclosed regarding lead?

A) Any lead present in drinking water

B) Any lead in the soil on the property

C) Any lead-based paint hazards known to the seller

D) Any lead in the neighboring properties

130. When it comes to material facts and defect disclosure, what should a seller prioritize?

A) Only disclosing major defects

B) Disclosing all known issues, regardless of significance

C) Hiding defects to ensure a quick sale

D) Disclosing defects only if asked by the buyer

131. Which of the following would likely require disclosure as a material fact or defect?

A) Recent upgrades to the property

B) A history of termite infestation

C) Regular maintenance of the HVAC system

D) A fresh coat of paint on the exterior walls

132. In the context of property condition, what might trigger inquiries about public or private land use controls?

A) Planned construction of a new mall nearby

B) Replacement of old carpeting in the house

C) Installation of new light fixtures

D) Repainting the exterior of the property

133. Which environmental issue should be disclosed to potential buyers to comply with regulations?

A) Recent landscaping improvements

B) Presence of radon gas

C) A well-maintained lawn

D) Installation of energy-efficient windows

134. What does the term "material facts" refer to in real estate disclosure?

A) Information that is irrelevant to the property

B) Information that may impact a buyer's decision

C) Information that only benefits the seller

D) Information that the seller is not obligated to disclose

135. What is an example of a defect that should be disclosed to potential buyers?

A) Recent painting of the interior walls

B) A history of roof repairs

C) Regular servicing of the plumbing system

D) Upgraded kitchen appliances

136. Which environmental issue would typically require disclosure?

A) Recent lawn fertilization

B) Presence of mold in the basement

C) Installation of new light fixtures

D) Aesthetic improvements to the landscaping

137. What is the primary purpose of government disclosure requirements related to lead?

A) To protect sellers from liability

B) To inform buyers about potential health risks

C) To increase property values

D) To promote environmental conservation

138. In the context of property condition, what would be considered a material fact?

A) Recent changes to the property's exterior paint color

B) A history of flooding in the basement

C) Regular maintenance of the landscaping

D) Installation of a new security system

139. What type of environmental issue should be disclosed to potential buyers?

A) A recent inspection for termites

B) A history of neighborhood noise complaints

C) A well-maintained septic system

D) Installation of new energy-efficient appliances

140. Which of the following is an example of a defect that should be disclosed?

A) A freshly painted exterior

B) Presence of a cracked foundation

C) Upgraded bathroom fixtures

D) Installation of new hardwood flooring

141. Which of the following are requirements for the validity of a contract?

A) Offer and acceptance

B) Consideration

C) Legal capacity

D) All of the above

142. What factors can affect the enforceability of contracts?

A) Duress

B) Undue influence

C) Misrepresentation

D) All of the above

143. Which type of contract is considered voidable?

A) A contract lacking consideration

B) A contract entered into under duress

C) A contract lacking legal capacity

D) A contract lacking offer and acceptance

144. When are contracts considered executed?

A) When all parties have signed the agreement

B) When all terms of the contract have been fulfilled

C) When the contract is ready for signature

D) When the contract is delivered to the parties

145. Which action signifies acceptance of a contract?

A) Counteroffer

B) Revocation

C) Rejection

D) Signing the contract

146. What remedies are available for breach of contract?

A) Rescission

B) Specific performance

C) Damages

D) All of the above

147. Under what circumstance may a contract be terminated?

A) By agreement of the parties

B) By breach of contract

C) By operation of law

D) All of the above

148. Which of the following is true regarding electronic signatures and paperless transactions?

A) They are not legally binding

B) They are only valid in certain states

C) They are governed by federal law

D) They are legally equivalent to traditional signatures in many situations

149. What distinguishes a bilateral contract from a unilateral contract?

A) The number of parties involved

B) The type of consideration offered

C) The mode of acceptance required

D) The presence of an offer and acceptance

150. When does an offer become binding?

A) When it is communicated to the offeree

B) When it is signed by the offeror

C) When consideration is exchanged

D) When the offeree accepts the offer

151. What is the significance of "time is of the essence" clause in a purchase agreement?

A) It allows for an extension of the closing date

B) It makes punctual performance an essential term of the contract

C) It renders the contract voidable

D) It prohibits the use of contingencies

152. What happens if a buyer makes a counteroffer to the seller's initial offer?

A) The original offer is terminated

B) The seller must accept the counteroffer

C) The buyer must accept the seller's initial offer

D) Both parties are bound by their respective offers

153. In a multiple offer situation, what is the responsibility of the seller's agent?

A) Present all offers to the seller

B) Advise the seller to accept the highest offer

C) Disclose the terms of all offers to all buyers

D) Disclose only the highest offer to the seller

154. What is a common contingency in a purchase agreement?

A) Seller financing approval

B) Home inspection

C) Landlord approval

D) Mortgage insurance approval

155. How can a contract be rescinded?

A) By mutual agreement of the parties

B) By operation of law

C) By revocation of offer

D) By rejection of the offer

156. Which of the following is NOT a type of lease commonly used in property management?

A) Percentage lease

B) Gross lease

C) Shared lease

D) Net lease

157. What are the key elements of a lease agreement?

A) Lessee's responsibilities only

B) Lessor's responsibilities only

C) Terms of the lease, rent amount, and signatures of both parties

D) Lease duration and property description only

158. In a net lease, which of the following is typically the responsibility of the tenant?

A) Property taxes

B) Property insurance

C) Maintenance expenses

D) All of the above

159. What is a property manager's fiduciary responsibility?

A) To prioritize their own interests above the landlord's

B) To act in the best interest of the landlord

C) To maximize profits regardless of tenant satisfaction

D) To disclose confidential information to tenants

160. Which federal law prohibits discrimination in housing based on race, color, religion, sex, disability, familial status, or national origin?

A) Americans with Disabilities Act (ADA)

B) Fair Housing Act

C) Equal Credit Opportunity Act (ECOA)

D) Housing and Urban Development Act (HUDA)

161. **A property manager is responsible for ensuring ADA compliance. What does ADA stand for?**

A) American Disability Association

B) Accessibility and Disability Act

C) Americans with Disabilities Act

D) Association for Disability Awareness

162. **Under the Fair Housing Act, which of the following is considered a protected characteristic?**

A) Age

B) Marital status

C) Military status

D) All of the above

163. **Which of the following is an example of a ground lease?**

A) A lease for office space within a shopping mall

B) A lease for agricultural land

C) A lease for a residential apartment

D) A lease for a warehouse space

164. **What is the primary duty of a property manager?**

A) To maximize rent collection

B) To minimize expenses

C) To act in the best interest of the property owner

D) To attract new tenants

165. **Which of the following is NOT typically included in a lease agreement?**

A) Rent amount and due date

B) Description of property

C) Tenant's favorite color

D) Signatures of both parties

166. **In which type of lease does the tenant pay a base rent plus a percentage of their monthly sales?**

A) Gross lease

B) Net lease

C) Percentage lease

D) Ground lease

167. Under the Fair Housing Act, what is the maximum fine for a first-time violator?

A) $10,000

C) $50,000

B) $25,000

D) $75,000

168. What does the Fair Housing Act prohibit landlords from doing?

A) Rejecting a rental application based on race

C) Charging higher rent based on national origin

B) Providing special privileges to certain tenants based on religion

D) All of the above

169. Which of the following is NOT a responsibility of a property manager's fiduciary duty?

A) Acting in the best interest of the tenant

C) Avoiding conflicts of interest

B) Disclosing material facts to the property owner

D) Maintaining confidentiality

170. What is the purpose of the Americans with Disabilities Act (ADA) in property management?

A) To ensure fair housing practices

C) To ensure accessibility for individuals with disabilities

B) To promote energy efficiency

D) To regulate rental rates

171. Which of the following is typically insured against in title insurance?

A) Market value fluctuations

C) Encumbrances and defects in title

B) Environmental hazards

D) Property tax assessments

172. What are some common components of a title search?

A) Property appraisal, zoning analysis, and land use assessment

B) Title insurance policy review, mortgage approval, and tax assessment

C) Title searches, title abstracts, and examination of the chain of title

D) Property survey, easement identification, and utility assessment

173. What distinguishes a marketable title from an insurable title?

A) Marketable title refers to a title without defects, while insurable title refers to a title that can be insured against defects

B) Marketable title refers to a title with defects that can be resolved, while insurable title refers to a title without defects

C) Marketable title refers to a title that cannot be insured, while insurable title refers to a title that can be insured

D) Marketable title refers to a title that cannot be transferred, while insurable title refers to a title that can be transferred

174. Which of the following is a potential title problem that may arise?

A) Property appreciation

B) Clear chain of title

C) Encumbrances such as liens or easements

D) Transparent property boundaries

175. At what point does title typically pass in a real estate transaction?

A) Upon signing the purchase agreement

B) Upon acceptance of the offer

C) Upon recording the deed

D) Upon completion of the home inspection

176. What is the primary purpose of recording a deed?

A) To ensure the buyer's eligibility for a mortgage

B) To establish the seller's ownership of the property

C) To provide public notice of property ownership

D) To expedite the closing process

177. In a real estate transaction, what are prorated items typically related to?

A) Property taxes and insurance premiums

B) Title insurance and appraisal fees

C) Realtor commissions and attorney fees

D) Home inspection and repair costs

178. What do TRID disclosures provide information about?

A) Property tax assessments

B) Mortgage loan terms and costs

C) Homeowner association fees

D) Home warranty coverage

179. When estimating closing costs, which of the following would NOT typically be considered?

A) Property taxes

B) Real estate agent commissions

C) Homeowner association fees

D) Title insurance premiums

180. What is the primary purpose of a home or construction warranty program?

A) To insure against property damage caused by natural disasters

B) To provide coverage for routine maintenance and repairs

C) To guarantee the structural integrity of a newly constructed home

D) To protect against loss of income due to property defects

181. What is the scope of a home or construction warranty program typically?

A) Coverage for personal property only

B) Limited to structural defects for a specific period

C) Comprehensive coverage for all property-related issues

D) Coverage for natural disasters and environmental hazards

182. What is the process of taking back a mortgaged property when the mortgagor fails to keep up mortgage payments called?

A) Mortgage restructuring

B) Deed in lieu of foreclosure

C) Foreclosure

D) Pre-foreclosure

183. In a short sale, what happens to the proceeds from the sale?

A) They go to the homeowner

B) They are distributed among creditors

C) They are used to pay off the remaining mortgage balance

D) They are exempt from taxation

184. What is the primary responsibility of an escrow agent?

A) To represent the seller's interests in a real estate transaction

B) To ensure all parties fulfill their contractual obligations

C) To conduct property appraisals and inspections

D) To provide financing for the buyer

185. When is a warranty deed typically used?

A) In a foreclosure sale

B) In a short sale transaction

C) When the seller wants to provide maximum protection to the buyer

D) When transferring property between family members

186. Which type of deed provides the least amount of protection to the buyer regarding the condition of the title?

A) Warranty deed

B) Quitclaim deed

C) Special warranty deed

D) Bargain and sale deed

187. What is a quitclaim deed primarily used for?

A) Transferring ownership between family members

B) Guaranteeing clear title to the buyer

C) Providing warranties against title defects

D) Establishing the purchase price of the property

188. When does the responsibility for property taxes typically transfer in a real estate transaction?

A) Upon signing the purchase agreement

B) Upon closing

C) Upon recording the deed

D) Upon completion of the home inspection

189. What is the purpose of prorating property taxes in a real estate transaction?

A) To ensure the buyer pays all outstanding property taxes

B) To fairly divide property tax expenses between the buyer and seller

C) To exempt the property from future tax assessments

D) To reduce the overall closing costs for the buyer

190. Which statement regarding property taxes is true?

A) Property taxes are determined by the mortgage lender.

B) Property tax assessments are based on the market value of the property.

C) Property taxes are typically paid on a quarterly basis.

D) Property tax rates are consistent across all jurisdictions.

191. **In a real estate transaction, what do closing statements typically include?**

A) Final property inspection reports

B) Mortgage loan application forms

C) Itemized lists of all financial transactions related to the sale

D) Homeowner association bylaws

192. **What is the primary purpose of TRID disclosures?**

A) To provide information about property tax assessments

B) To ensure compliance with zoning regulations

C) To disclose the terms and costs of a mortgage loan to the borrower

D) To establish the purchase price of the property

193. **When estimating closing costs, what is typically NOT included?**

A) Title insurance premiums

B) Attorney fees

C) Homeowner association dues

D) Realtor commissions

194. **What is the primary purpose of a home warranty program?**

A) To protect against natural disasters

B) To provide coverage for routine maintenance

C) To guarantee the structural integrity of a newly constructed home

D) To insure against property damage caused by tenants

195. **What does the scope of a home warranty program typically cover?**

A) Structural defects only

B) All property-related issues

C) Routine maintenance and repairs

D) Natural disasters and environmental hazards

196. In a foreclosure process, what is the role of the lender?

A) To sell the property to recover the outstanding loan balance

B) To assist the homeowner in finding alternative financing options

C) To renegotiate the terms of the mortgage agreement

D) To pay off the homeowner's debt

197. What is a short sale in real estate?

A) A sale where the property is sold for more than the outstanding mortgage balance

B) A sale where the property is sold for less than the outstanding mortgage balance

C) A sale where the property is sold without a real estate agent

D) A sale where the property is sold through an auction

198. What is the primary responsibility of an escrow agent?

A) To represent the buyer's interests in a real estate transaction

B) To facilitate the transfer of funds and documents between parties

C) To conduct property inspections and appraisals

D) To provide financing for the seller

199. What is the purpose of a warranty deed?

A) To transfer ownership of real property

B) To provide warranties against title defects

C) To guarantee the structural integrity of a newly constructed home

D) To establish the purchase price of the property

200. What type of deed provides the greatest level of protection to the buyer regarding the condition of the title?

A) Warranty deed

B) Quitclaim deed

C) Special warranty deed

D) Bargain and sale deed

201. What is the primary purpose of trust accounts in real estate transactions?

A) To maximize profits for the real estate agency

B) To ensure transparency in financial transactions

C) To hold client funds securely

D) To avoid paying taxes on earned commissions

202. What term refers to the illegal practice of mixing personal funds with client funds in a trust account?

A) Escrow fraud

B) Embezzlement

C) Conversion

D) Commingling

203. Which of the following is NOT a protected class under federal fair housing laws?

A) Race

B) Religion

C) Sexual orientation

D) Disability

204. What conduct is prohibited under federal fair housing laws as it relates to real estate transactions?

A) Redlining

B) Blockbusting

C) Steering

D) All of the above

205. The Americans with Disabilities Act (ADA) prohibits discrimination against individuals with disabilities in which areas?

A) Employment

B) Housing

C) Public accommodations

D) All of the above

206. Which of the following is an exemption to federal fair housing laws?

A) Age

B) Gender

C) National origin

D) Familial status

207. What is required in real estate advertising to ensure compliance with truth in advertising regulations?

A) Use of exaggerated claims

B) Accurate and truthful representations

C) Hiding negative property features

D) Use of ambiguous language

208. What is the primary purpose of technology regulations in real estate?

A) To prevent the use of modern technology

B) To protect consumer privacy and confidential information

C) To limit access to property listings

D) To increase advertising costs

209. What is the purpose of the Do-Not-Call List in real estate?

A) To prevent telemarketing calls to potential clients

B) To promote cold calling for real estate agents

C) To restrict access to property information

D) To increase advertising revenue

210. Which of the following best describes the responsibilities of a real estate licensee as an independent contractor?

A) They have control over their work hours and methods.

B) They are considered employees of the brokerage.

C) They have limited authority in negotiating contracts.

D) They are not responsible for maintaining confidentiality.

211. What is the term for the level of care and diligence that a real estate licensee must exercise in representing their clients?

A) Negligence

B) Due diligence

C) Standard of care

D) Breach of duty

212. What is the purpose of antitrust laws in real estate?

A) To prevent unfair competition

B) To increase brokerage fees

C) To limit property listings

D) To encourage price fixing

213. Which of the following is considered an antitrust violation in real estate?

A) Price fixing

B) Truthful advertising

C) Fair housing compliance

D) Confidentiality agreements

214. What is the responsibility of a real estate agent regarding trust accounts?

A) To use the funds for personal expenses

B) To deposit client funds into a trust account

C) To transfer trust funds to their personal account

D) To invest trust funds in the stock market

215. Which of the following is a protected class under federal fair housing laws?

A) Occupation

B) Age

C) Political affiliation

D) Credit score

216. Which advertising practice violates fair housing laws by targeting specific racial or ethnic groups?

A) Redlining

B) Blockbusting

C) Steering

D) Reverse mortgage advertising

217. What is the primary purpose of the Americans with Disabilities Act (ADA) in real estate?

A) To prevent discrimination based on religion

B) To improve accessibility for individuals with disabilities

C) To regulate real estate advertis

D) To enforce age restrictions in housing

218. Which of the following is NOT an exemption to federal fair housing laws?

A) Age

B) Religion

C) National origin

D) Disability

219. What is required for real estate advertising to comply with truth in advertising regulations?

A) Accurate and truthful representations

B) Use of deceptive language

C) Concealment of property defects

D) Exaggerated claims

220. What is the purpose of technology regulations in real estate?

A) To protect consumer privacy

B) To increase advertising costs

C) To limit access to property listings

D) To prevent the use of modern technology

221. What is the primary purpose of the Do-Not-Call List in real estate?

A) To prevent telemarketing calls

B) To promote cold calling

C) To restrict access to property information

D) To increase advertising revenue

222. What distinguishes a real estate licensee as an independent contractor?

A) Control over work hours and methods

B) Employee status with the brokerage

C) Limited authority in contract negotiations

D) Shared responsibility for confidentiality

223. What level of care and diligence must a real estate licensee exercise in representing clients?

A) Due diligence

B) Negligence

C) Standard of care

D) Breach of duty

224. What is the primary purpose of antitrust laws in real estate?

A) To prevent unfair competition

B) To increase brokerage fees

C) To limit property listings

D) To encourage price fixing

225. Which practice is an antitrust violation in real estate?

A) Price fixing

B) Truthful advertising

C) Fair housing compliance

D) Confidentiality agreements

226. What is a real estate agent's responsibility regarding trust accounts?

A) Deposit client funds into a trust account

B) Use funds for personal expenses

C) Transfer trust funds to a personal account

D) Invest trust funds in the stock market

227. Which is a protected class under federal fair housing laws?

A) Occupation

B) Age

C) Political affiliation

D) Credit score

228. What advertising practice violates fair housing laws by targeting specific racial or ethnic groups?

A) Redlining

B) Blockbusting

C) Steering

D) Reverse mortgage advertising

229. What is the primary purpose of the Americans with Disabilities Act (ADA) in real estate?

A) Prevent discrimination based on religion

B) Improve accessibility for individuals with disabilities

C) Regulate real estate advertising

D) Enforce age restrictions in housing

230. Which of the following is NOT an exemption to federal fair housing laws?

A) Age

C) National origin

B) Religion

D) Disability

231. What is the loan-to-value ratio if a buyer purchases a property for $200,000 with a down payment of $40,000?

A) 20%

C) 30%

B) 25%

D) 35%

232. If a borrower pays 2 discount points on a loan of $150,000, how much is the discount in dollars?

A) $2,000

C) $4,000

B) $3,000

D) $5,000

233. What is the equity of a homeowner whose property is valued at $300,000 with a mortgage balance of $180,000?

A) $60,000

C) $120,000

B) $90,000

D) $150,000

234. If a homebuyer makes a down payment of $30,000 on a property valued at $200,000, how much will they finance?

A) $150,000

C) $180,000

B) $170,000

D) $190,000

235. What is the property tax amount for a property assessed at $250,000 with a tax rate of 1.5%?

A) $2,500

C) $3,750

B) $3,250

D) $4,250

236. If a property sells for $300,000, and the listing agent's commission is 5%, how much is the commission?

A) $12,000

B) $13,500

C) $15,000

D) $16,500

237. What are the seller's proceeds if a property sells for $400,000, the seller owes $250,000 on their mortgage, and they pay a 6% commission?

A) $90,000

B) $100,000

C) $110,000

D) $120,000

238. If a buyer purchases a property for $250,000 with a 20% down payment, how much are their funds needed at closing, assuming closing costs of $7,500?

A) $42,500

B) $50,000

C) $57,500

D) $65,000

239. What is the transfer fee for a property sold for $350,000 in a state with a 1.5% transfer tax rate?

A) $3,500

B) $5,250

C) $7,000

D) $8,750

240. If a homeowner's monthly PITI payment is $1,800, and $300 goes towards property taxes and insurance combined, how much is the monthly principal and interest payment?

A) $1,200

B) $1,300

C) $1,400

D) $1,500

241. **A property is assessed at $180,000, and the property tax rate is 2.5%. How much is the annual property tax?**

A) $3,600

B) $4,500

C) $4,750

D) $5,250

242. **If a real estate agent earns a commission of $9,000 on a sale and the agreed commission split with their brokerage is 60/40, how much does the agent receive?**

A) $3,400

B) $4,200

C) $5,400

D) $6,000

243. **What is the loan-to-value ratio if a buyer finances $120,000 for a property valued at $150,000?**

A) 60%

B) 70%

C) 80%

D) 90%

244. **If a buyer purchases a property for $280,000 and puts 15% down, how much is their down payment?**

A) $35,000

B) $42,000

C) $45,000

D) $49,000

245. **A property sells for $350,000, and the seller pays 1.5% of the sales price in transfer fees. How much are the transfer fees?**

A) $3,500

B) $5,250

C) $6,000

D) $7,000

246. If a property sells for $400,000, and the seller's mortgage payoff is $250,000, what are the seller's net proceeds after paying a 6% commission?

A) $110,000

B) $115,000

C) $120,000

D) $125,000

247. What are the monthly principal and interest payments on a mortgage of $200,000 with an interest rate of 4.5% for 30 years?

A) $1,013.37

B) $1,054.37

C) $1,096.37

D) $1,137.37

248. A property sells for $300,000, and the buyer finances $240,000. What is the loan-to-value ratio?

A) 70%

B) 75%

C) 80%

D) 85%

249. If a property has annual property taxes of $3,600 and the tax rate is 2.5%, what is the property's assessed value?

A) $120,000

B) $144,000

C) $150,000

D) $180,000

250. What is the monthly PITI payment on a mortgage of $180,000 with an interest rate of 5% for 25 years, including property taxes and insurance of $200 per month?

A) $1,260

B) $1,350

C) $1,440

D) $1,530

251. A valid exclusive listing, has to include always ?

A) Permissions for the listing broker

B) a definitive date of expiration

C) an automatic renewal clause

D) a forfeiture clause

Answers

1.   C) House

2.   C) To define the boundaries of real property

3.   C) Metes and bounds

4.   C) Mineral rights

5.   B) Mortgage

6.   C) Tenancy in common

7.   C) Timeshare

8.   D) Encroachment

9.   C) Ownership in severalty

10.   C) Ownership for the lifetime of the owner or another designated person

11.   B) Joint tenancy

12.   B) Lien

13.   C) Condominium

14.   B) To divide land into townships and sections

15.   A) Livable area

16.   B) Cooperative

17.   D) Rectangular survey system

18.   D) To grant limited use of property to another party

19.   A) Lien

20.   C) Tenancy by the entirety

21.   C) Easement

22.   B) Eminent domain

23.   C) Deed restrictions

24.   B) Zoning ordinances

25.   B) Condemnation

26.   C) Environmental hazards

27.   C) Zoning regulations

28.   D) Deed restriction

29.   B) To ensure public safety and welfare

30.   C) Zoning ordinances

31.   C) Eminent domain

32.   C) Deed restriction

33.   A) Zoning

34.   C) Zoning ordinance

35.   C) Zoning ordinances

36.   C) Deed restriction

37.   D) Zoning ordinance

38.   B) Zoning

39.   C) Zoning ordinance

40.   A) Zoning

41.   B) To estimate the market value of a property

42.   C) Property marketing

43.   B) When refinancing a mortgage

44.   D) Location

45.   A) Sales or market comparison approach

46.   C) Calculating the cost to replace the property

47.   B) Income analysis approach

48.   B) Gross Rent Multiplier

49.   B) Gross Income ÷ Property Value

50.   C) Replacement cost

51.   B) For historic properties with unique features

52.   C) Income analysis approach

53.   B) The rate of return an investor expects from the property

54.   A) It considers only the gross rental income of a property.

55.   C) Physical condition

56.   A) Sales or market comparison approach

57.   B) Its overall market value

58.   A) Properties with similar characteristics that are used to estimate the value of a subject property

59.   C) Sales or market comparison approach

60.   C) Capitalization

61.   B) Loan to Value

62.   B) Private Mortgage Insurance

63.   B) Principal, Interest, Taxes, Insurance

64.   C) Interest

65. C) Principal, Interest, Taxes, and Insurance

66. C) Mortgage

67. C) FHA Insured Loan

68. B) The loan balance decreases over time through regular payments

69. B) The interest rate adjusts periodically based on market conditions

70. C) Contract for Deed

71. C) Underwriting

72. B) Truth in Lending Act (TILA)

73. B) Real Estate Settlement Procedures Act

74. C) Equal Credit Opportunity Act (ECOA)

75. B) Debt ratios

76. C) To protect consumers by requiring clear disclosure of loan terms and costs

77. C) Consumer Finance Protection Bureau/TILA-RESPA Integrated Disclosures

78. C) To provide consumers with information about closing costs and eliminate kickbacks

79. C) Vehicle ownership

80. A) Loan to Value

81. B) Must have a steady income source

82. B) Balloon payment

83. C) 36%

84. C) Equal Credit Opportunity Act

85. B) To assess the borrower's creditworthiness based on their credit history

86. B) To regulate financial institutions and protect consumers in the financial marketplace

87. B) Real Estate Settlement Procedures Act (RESPA)

88. B) To provide temporary financing until permanent financing can be arranged

89. A) Property value

90. C) Consumer Financial Protection Bureau

91. C) Non-agent

92. C) Accountability

93. B) Duties of the agent

94. D) After a specified period of time

95. B) Loyalty

96. B) Transactional

97. D) Bankruptcy of the agent

98. B) Honesty

99. C) Dual agency

100. C) Confidentiality

101. D) Commission structure

102. A) Upon the expiration of the specified term

103. D) When the property is destroyed

104. A) Loyalty

105. D) Principal-agent

106. C) Disclosure

107.   D) Death of the principal

108.   B) Disclosure

109.   A) Facilitator

110.   D) Mutual agreement

111.   C) Obedience

112.   D) Completion of the transaction

113.   C) Dual agency

114.   C) Honesty

115.   B) Non-agent

116.   C) Dual agency

117.   C) Confidentiality

118.   D) Commission structure

119.   C) Disclosure

120.   D) Non-agent

121.   C) Suspected mold growth

122.   C) When proposed uses or changes in uses are anticipated

123.   B) Presence of asbestos

124.   C) Lead-based paint disclosure

125.   B) Any information that might impact the property's value or desirability

126.   B) A leaking roof

127.   D) A recent increase in property taxes

128.   B) Presence of lead-based paint

129.   B) Any lead-based paint hazards known to the seller

130.   B) Disclosing all known issues, regardless of significance

131.   B) A history of termite infestation

132.   A) Planned construction of a new mall nearby

133.   B) Presence of radon gas

134.   B) Information that may impact a buyer's decision

135.   B) A history of roof repairs

136.   B) Presence of mold in the basement

137.   B) To inform buyers about potential health risks

138.   B) A history of flooding in the basement

139.   B) A history of neighborhood noise complaints

140.   B) Presence of a cracked foundation

141.   D) All of the above

142.   D) All of the above

143.   B) A contract entered into under duress

144.   B) When all terms of the contract have been fulfilled

145.   D) Signing the contract

146.   D) All of the above

147.   D) All of the above

148.   D) They are legally equivalent to traditional signatures in many situations

149.   D) The presence of an offer and acceptance

150.   D) When the offeree accepts the offer

151.   B) It makes punctual performance an essential term of the contract

152.   A) The original offer is terminated

153.   A) Present all offers to the seller

154.   B) Home inspection

155.   A) By mutual agreement of the parties

156.   C) Shared lease

157.   C) Terms of the lease, rent amount, and signatures of both parties

158.   D) All of the above

159.   B) To act in the best interest of the landlord

160.   B) Fair Housing Act

161.   C) Americans with Disabilities Act

162.   D) All of the above

163.   B) A lease for agricultural land

164.   C) To act in the best interest of the property owner

165.   C) Tenant's favorite color

166.   C) Percentage lease

167.   B) $25,000

168.   D) All of the above

169.   A) Acting in the best interest of the tenant

170.   C) To ensure accessibility for individuals with disabilities

171.   C) Encumbrances and defects in title

172.   C) Title searches, title abstracts, and examination of the chain of title

173. A) Marketable title refers to a title without defects, while insurable title refers to a title that can be insured against defects

174. C) Encumbrances such as liens or easements

175. C) Upon recording the deed

176. C) To provide public notice of property ownership

177. A) Property taxes and insurance premiums

178. B) Mortgage loan terms and costs

179. C) Homeowner association fees

180. C) To guarantee the structural integrity of a newly constructed home

181. B) Limited to structural defects for a specific period

182. C) Foreclosure

183. C) They are used to pay off the remaining mortgage balance

184. B) To ensure all parties fulfill their contractual obligations

185. C) When the seller wants to provide maximum protection to the buyer

186. B) Quitclaim deed

187. A) Transferring ownership between family members

188. B) Upon closing

189. B) To fairly divide property tax expenses between the buyer and seller

190. B) Property tax assessments are based on the market value of the property.

191. C) Itemized lists of all financial transactions related to the sale

192. C) To disclose the terms and costs of a mortgage loan to the borrower

193. C) Homeowner association dues

194. B) To provide coverage for routine maintenance

195. C) Routine maintenance and repairs

196. A) To sell the property to recover the outstanding loan balance

197. B) A sale where the property is sold for less than the outstanding mortgage balance

198. B) To facilitate the transfer of funds and documents between parties

199. A) To transfer ownership of real property

200. A) Warranty deed

201. C) To hold client funds securely

202. D) Commingling

203. C) Sexual orientation

204. D) All of the above

205. D) All of the above

206. A) Age

207. B) Accurate and truthful representations

208. B) To protect consumer privacy and confidential information

209. A) To prevent telemarketing calls to potential clients

210. A) They have control over their work hours and methods.

211. C) Standard of care

212. A) To prevent unfair competition

213. A) Price fixing

214. B) To deposit client funds into a trust account

215.   B) Age

216.   C) Steering

217.   B) To improve accessibility for individuals with disabilities

218.   B) Religion

219.   A) Accurate and truthful representations

220.   A) To protect consumer privacy

221.   A) To prevent telemarketing calls

222.   A) Control over work hours and methods

223.   C) Standard of care

224.   A) To prevent unfair competition

225.   A) Price fixing

226.   A) Deposit client funds into a trust account

227.   B) Age

228.   C) Steering

229.   B) Improve accessibility for individuals with disabilities

230.   B) Religion

231.   B) 25%

232.   C) $4,000

233.   B) $90,000

234.   A) $150,000

235.   C) $3,750

236.   C) $15,000

237. B) $100,000

238. C) $57,500

239. B) $5,250

240. C) $1,400

241. B) $4,500

242. C) $5,400

243. C) 80%

244. C) $42,000

245. D) $5,250

246. B) $115,000

247. A) $1,013.37

248. C) 80%

249. B) $144,000

250. C) $1,440

251. B) a definite date of expiration

Answers/Solutions to the Exercise Questions

Chapter 1

1. Given:

   Length of land = 300 feet

   Width of land = 500 feet

   Using the formula provided:

   Total Area (in acres) = Length (ft) x Width (ft) / 43,560

   Substituting the given values:

   Total Area = (300 feet x 500 feet) / 43,560 square feet

   Total Area = 150,000 square feet / 43,560 square feet/acre

   Total Area ≈ 3.44 acres (≈ means approximately)

   So, the total area of the land is approximately 3.44 acres.

2. **Livable area** = 1,800 square feet

   Total rentable area = 2,200 square feet

   Using the given formula:

   Unusable Space (%) = (1 – livable area/rentable areA) x 100%

   Substituting the given values:

   Unusable Space (%) = (1 – 1,800/2,200) x 100%

   Unusable Space (%) = (1 – 0.818) x 100%

   Unusable Space (%) ≈ (0.182) x 100%

   Unusable Space (%) ≈ 18.2%

   So, the percentage of unusable space in the property is approximately 18.2%.

3. When a homeowner grants another person the right to live in their house for the duration of their lifetime, it is known as a **Life Estate**. In a life estate, the life tenant has the right to use and enjoy the property during their lifetime, but ownership of the property goes back to the original owner or passes to a remainderman upon the death of the life tenant.

Chapter 2

1. **Property Tax** = $300,000 (Assessed Value) × 1.5% (Tax Rate)

   Property Tax = $4,500

2. Zoning laws may restrict the operation of a small retail store in a residential area, necessitating **compliance** through permits, adherence to ordinances, and possible variances.

3. Properties near former industrial sites can present environmental hazards such as **contamination from pollutants**, requiring measures like environmental assessments, and remediation, coupled with compliance with safety measures.

Chapter 3

1. For the property generating $150,000 in gross annual rental income and priced at $1,200,000:

   GRM = Price / Gross Annual Rental Income

   GRM = $1,200,000 / $150,000

   GRM = 8

2. For the property generating $150,000 in gross annual income and priced at $2,250,000:

   GIM = Price / Gross Annual Income

   GIM = $2,250,000 / $150,000

   GIM = 15

3. Given that the GRM of a property is 8 and its gross annual rental income is $80,000.

   We know that,

   Purchase Price = GRM x Gross Annual Rental Income

   Purchase Price = 8 x $80,000

   Purchase Price = $640,000

4. Given that the GIM of a property is 12 and its gross annual income is $180,000.

   Purchase Price = GIM * Gross Annual Income

   Purchase Price = 12 * $180,000

   Purchase Price = $2,160,000

Chapter 4

A. Basic Concepts & Terminologies

Here's how to calculate the upfront payment for each option.

Option A:

Upfront payment = $300,000 * 0.03

Upfront payment = $9,000

Option B:

Upfront payment = $300,000 * 0.05

Upfront payment = $15,000

Now, to find the lower monthly mortgage payment, you need to calculate the monthly payments for each option using the respective interest rates.

Monthly **Payment= P * [r * (1 + r)^n] / [(1 + r)^n – 1]**

("^" indicates exponentiation/power given to the value within the brackets prior to it)

where:

M = monthly payment

P = principal loan amount

r = monthly interest rate (annual rate / 12)

n = number of payments (loan term in years * 12)

For Option A:

r = 4.5% / 12 = 0.045 / 12

r = 0.00375

Now,

n = loan term in years * 12

n = 30 * 12

n = 360 months

For Option B:

r = 4.0% / 12

r = 0.04 / 12

r= 0.00333

Now, by putting these values into the monthly payment formula for each option and after comparing the results, we can find out the preferred option (the one which is low). Let's calculate:

For Option A:

r = 0.00375 (monthly interest rate)

n = 360 (number of payments)

By using the formula:

Monthly Payment= P * [r * (1+r)^n] / [(1+r)^n – 1]

$M_A = 300{,}000 * [.00375 * (1 + .00375)^{360}] / [(1 + 0.00375)^{360} – 1]$

('*' & 'x' refer to multiplication)

$M_A \approx 1{,}520.06$

For Option B:

$M_B = 300{,}000 * [.00333 * (1 + .00333)^{360}] / [(1 + 0.00333)^{360} – 1]$

$M_B \approx 1{,}432.25$

Option B has a lower monthly payment, making it the preferred choice for minimizing the monthly mortgage payment.

Chapter 5

1. **Commission** = $300,000 × 5%

    Commission = $15,000

2. (A) Principal-Agent

3. (D) **Mutual** agreement

Chapter 8

1. A lease in which the landlord pays all or most of the property expenses, including taxes, insurance, and maintenance is called a **gross lease**. For example, a tenant renting a commercial space for $2,000 per month with the landlord covering all property expenses.

2. ***Total Rent = Base Rent + Property Taxes + Insurance***

    Total Rent = $1,500 (Base Rent) + $200 (Property Taxes) + $100 (Insurance)

    Total Rent = $1,500 + $200 + $100

    Total Rent = $1,800 per month

3. A property manager misuses funds from the property's rental income for personal expenses instead of using them for property maintenance or owner distributions, thereby breaching their duty of loyalty and care to the property owner.

Chapter 9

1. **Marketable title** signifies a clear ownership free from defects, while **insurable title**, although may have minor issues, is still insurable, both essential for property transfer in real estate transactions.

2. **Recording a deed** is crucial as it publicly declares ownership, protects buyers from third-party claims, and establishes ownership priority.

3. **Closing statements** detail financial transactions, ensuring transparency, while **TRID disclosures** provide borrowers with clear mortgage terms and costs as required by law.

4. **Home or construction warranty programs** offer coverage for structural defects and major systems, providing financial protection to homeowners against unforeseen repair costs, thereby boosting confidence in property purchases.

Chapter 10

1. Protected classes under federal fair housing laws include race, color, national origin, religion, sex, familial status, and disability. Discrimination might occur if a landlord refuses to rent to a family with children (familial status) or if a seller refuses to sell to someone because of their race.

2. **Requirements** for handling confidential information include safeguarding client information, obtaining consent before sharing confidential details, and maintaining records securely. The **Do-Not-Call List** is for real estate marketers, stopping them from calling people who have registered their phone numbers on the list. Thus, limiting the use of telemarketing for lead generation.

Chapter 11

A. BASIC MATH CONCEPTS

1. LTV Ratio

*LTV Ratio = (Mortgage Loan Amount / Property Value) * 100%*

*LTV Ratio = ($230,000 / $300,000) * 100%*

LTV Ratio = 76.67%

Thus, they would be able to secure it as per the 80% rule.

4. Down payment

Down Payment = Property Price x Down Payment Percentage

Down Payment = $500,000 x 20%

Down Payment = $100,000

And,

Amount to be Financed = Property Price - Down Payment

Amount to be Financed = $500,000 - $100,000

Amount to be Financed = $400,000

B. CALCULATIONS FOR TRANSACTIONS

1. Property Tax Calculations

Annual Property Tax = Property Assessment × Tax Rate

By substituting the given values, we get:

Annual Property Tax = $350,000 × 2%

Annual Property Tax = $7,000

3. Commissions and Commission Splits

Total commission = Property price × Commission rate

Total commission = $500,000 × 3%

Total commission = $15,000

Commission earned by buyer's agent (assuming 50/50 split) = Total commission ÷ 2

Commission earned by buyer's agent = $15,000 ÷ 2 = **$7,500**

4. Seller's Proceeds

Calculate the commission paid to the real estate agent:

Commission = Selling price * Commission rate

= $400,000 * 5%

Commission = $20,000

Add extra closing costs:

Total closing costs = Commission + Extra closing costs

= $20,000 + $10,000

Total Closing Costs = $30,000

Subtract total closing costs from the selling price:

Seller's proceeds = Selling price - Total closing costs

= $400,000 - $30,000

= $370,000

Therefore, the seller's proceeds of sale are **$370,000**.

5. Buyer's Funds Needed at Closing

To calculate the down payment amount:

Down payment = Property price x Down payment percentage

Down Payment = $650,000 * 20%

= $130,000

Now, add closing costs to the down payment:

Total funds needed = Down payment + Closing costs

= $130,000 + $10,000

= $140,000

So, the buyer needs **$140,000** at closing.

7. PITI

Total PITI = Principal + Interest + Property Taxes + Homeowner's Insurance

Total PITI = $1,200 + $800 + $300 + $100

Total PITI = $2,400

FREE BONUS

To get your free BONUS included with this guide please write an email to:

yourprepbook@gmail.com with "PSI National Real Estate License Exam Prep" in the subject line specifying your choice of bonus in the body of your email:

Bonus 1:   a real estate Math compendium with a lot of practice exercises

Bonus 2:   flashcards with additional 300 test questions to simulate exam experience.

1. Final preparation and Tips for the Exam Day

Preparation begins the night before. Ensure you have a good night's sleep—the kind that leaves you refreshed and mentally sharp. Avoid caffeinated beverages in the evening and try some light reading or a relaxation technique to help you drift off. Lay out your clothes and pack your bag with all necessary items (admission ticket, photo ID, water, snacks), so there's no morning rush.

The morning of the exam starts with a nutritious breakfast. Opt for foods known to aid cognitive function like eggs, which are rich in choline, or oatmeal which releases energy slowly—keeping hunger at bay and your mind focused. Check traffic reports and plan to arrive at the testing center early; aiming for at least 30 minutes before your scheduled start time eliminates unnecessary stress.

Once at the testing center, remain calm and proceed with check-in procedures outlined in the PSI Real Estate guidelines. Don't let last-minute cramming fluster you; trust in your preparation—this is not the time to flood your brain with new information. Instead, keep hydrated and focus on mindfulness or deep-breathing exercises to stay composed.

When the time comes to enter the examination room, make sure you use the restroom beforehand; this will help minimize disruptions during the exam. Find your allocated seat and set up your workstation according to the instructions—usually placing any belongings in a designated area away from other test-takers.

As you begin your exam, carefully read each question twice—rushing through can cause mistakes. Manage your time by gauging how long you spend on each question; if a question is too challenging or time-consuming, flag it and move on—you can return to it later with fresh eyes.

Throughout the exam maintain positive internal dialogue; remind yourself that you are prepared and capable. If anxiety creeps in, pause momentarily for some more deep-breathing exercises—they can work wonders for regaining composure.

Remember that some questions may be intentionally convoluted or tricky: they are designed to test not only knowledge but critical thinking skills as well. Utilize process-of-elimination techniques where possible—narrowing down choices increases your chance of selecting the correct answer.

When wrapping up, review flagged questions but avoid second-guessing yourself too often; initial instincts tend to be accurate more frequently than not. Scan through other answers if time allows—ensure everything has been answered and marked per instruction.

Once completed, take one last deep breath before submitting your test. Exit as directed by a proctor—and then exhale deeply; you've done all that you can do.

Whatever the outcome of today's exam might be, remember that navigating it successfully didn't only mean getting optimum answers but also managing yourself with confidence and calmness throughout. You're taking steps towards professional development that extend beyond mere test results—they're about personal growth and being ready to tackle challenges ahead with resilience.

And now, we are happy to share with you that you are ready for the exam. You know all there is to know about properties and real estate. But there are a few things that we would like you to follow to gain more control over your PSI exam. By gaining more control, we mean to nourish confidence within you which will eventually help you to prepare better, like a pro.

Let's take a look at them and then you will be allowed to go. You may choose to come back or revise sections where you think you lack.

7 Effective Strategies to Pass the Exam!

1. **Understand the Exam Format:** Familiarize yourself with the structure and format of the exam, including the number of questions, time constraints, and types of questions (multiple-choice, scenario-based, etc.). You can do this by going through questions and exercises that are given throughout the contents of this book.

2. **Create a Study Plan:** Develop a comprehensive study plan that covers all the topics outlined in the exam syllabus (outline of this book). Break down your study sessions into manageable tasks and allocate sufficient time to understand each topic thoroughly.

3. **Utilize Practice Exams:** Take advantage of practice exams given above to assess your understanding of the material and identify areas that need improvement.

4. **Focus on Weak Areas:** Once you are done with the initial preparation, think of areas where you feel that work is required. Then revise those topics. Also, don't neglect any aspect of the syllabus, but prioritize areas where you feel less confident.

5. **Engage in Active Learning:** Instead of passively reading through study materials, engage in active learning techniques such as summarizing key concepts, teaching the material to someone else, or creating flashcards. Actively engaging with the material enhances retention and understanding.

6. **Seek Clarification:** Don't hesitate to seek clarification on any confusing or unclear topics. Reach out to instructors, mentors, or fellow students for assistance. Utilize online forums or realtors' groups to discuss difficult concepts and gain insights from others.

7. **Take Care of Yourself:** While the exam is important, you need not go hard on yourself. You should prioritize self-care during your exam preparation. Focus on getting sufficient (7-8 hours) sleep, maintaining a healthy diet, and incorporating

regular breaks into your study routine. A well-rested and healthy mind performs better during exams.

The Three Golden Rules

In the end, we wish you good luck with these three golden rules that will further add to your assistance.

- **Preparation is Key:** Our minds perform better when it has some clarity in them. When we prepare diligently, cover the syllabus, and practice questions/exercises, that's when we equip ourselves with the knowledge and skills needed to tackle any question that comes our way.

- **Stay Calm and Focused:** Amidst the moments of great chaos and confusion, of exam day nerves, you should stay calm, and find your peace, so you can keep your focus fully charged. Try doing Yoga or stretching during preparatory sessions and see if you can notice any difference in your performance.

- **Trust Yourself:** Lastly, we must trust in our abilities. Through our dedication and hard work, we've earned the right to be confident in our knowledge. You should approach each question with conviction, knowing that you have given your best while preparing and are more than capable of overcoming any challenge.

2. Conclusion

As we conclude our journey through the comprehensive guide to ace the PSI Real Estate Exam, it's important to remember that becoming a certified agent not only enhances your skillset but also broadens your professional horizon. This book has equipped you with knowledge on everything from the exam structure, Real Estate laws and regulations, to mathematical guidance and ethic rules.

However, amongst all this technical know-how and strategies for exam success, the last piece of advice is perhaps the most crucial: believe in your ability to succeed. Your dedication to studying, understanding, and applying the myriad concepts required for certification is testament to your commitment to your future career.

CONCLUSIONS

In your final preparation phases, focus on areas you find challenging, but also ensure a well-rounded review of all chapters. Practice tests should have helped you identify these areas. Now is the time for targeted study sessions that transform weaknesses into strengths. Stay confident and manage your time wisely—nerves can be as significant an obstacle as any knowledge gap on the day of the exam.

Navigating the world of Real Estate is an ongoing learning experience even after passing the PSI Real Estate Exam. Keep up-to-date with new laws and technology changes that continuously shape the landscape. Embrace this calling with professionalism and ethical integrity; remember that at the core of your work are always your clients you assist positively through expertise and passion.

Go into your exam equipped not just with facts but with the assurance that you are ready. Good luck on your PSI Real Estate Exam and in your future career as a certified Real Estate agent.

THE END

Made in United States
Troutdale, OR
11/19/2024